RUSSIAN GROTESQUE REALISM

RUSSIAN GROTESQUE REALISM

The Great Reforms and the Gentry Decline

ANI KOKOBOBO

THE OHIO STATE UNIVERSITY PRESS
COLUMBUS

Library of Congress Cataloging-in-Publication Data
Names: Kokobobo, Ani, author.
Title: Russian grotesque realism : the great reforms and the gentry decline / Ani Kokobobo.
Description: Columbus : The Ohio State University Press, [2018] | Includes bibliographical references and index.
Identifiers: LCCN 2017045692 | ISBN 9780814213636 (cloth ; alk. paper) | ISBN 0814213634 (cloth ; alk. paper)
Subjects: LCSH: Russian fiction—19th century—History and criticism. | Grotesque in literature. | Realism in literature. | Gentry in literature.
Classification: LCC PG3096.G76 K65 2018 | DDC 891.73/08309—dc23
LC record available at https://lccn.loc.gov/2017045692

Cover design by Angela Moody
Text design by Juliet Williams
Type set in Adobe Minion Pro and ITC Officena

Studies of the Harriman Institute, Columbia University
The Harriman Institute, Columbia University, sponsors the Studies of the Harriman Institute in the belief that their publication contributes to scholarly research and public understanding. In this way the Institute, while not necessarily endorsing their conclusions, is pleased to make available the results of some of the research conducted under its auspices.

9 8 7 6 5 4 3 2 1

For John and Luke

CONTENTS

ACKNOWLEDGMENTS

This project has been many years in the making, and during its creation I have accrued many debts. I am deeply grateful to Liza Knapp for advising with grace and patience my study of the nineteenth-century Russian novel. I feel very fortunate to have found in her a mentor who helped me see the value of my ideas. As I have gone on to work in the field, I continue to look to her as a model of kindness, intellectual generosity, and professional ethics. I have relied many times on Irina Reyfman's mentorship, wisdom, and encyclopedic knowledge of Russian literature.

Several colleagues and friends in the profession have helped me in ways large and small by providing feedback on this book with various earlier iterations or by sharing their work at the opportune time. These include Valeria Sobol, Caryl Emerson, Kate Holland, Anne Lounsbery, Tom Newlin, Donna Orwin, Jeff Love, Michael Denner, William Mills Todd III, and Justin Weir. My colleagues in the Slavic department at the University of Kansas, Stephen Dickey and Vitaly Chernetsky, read and commented on my book proposal and helped me pitch it to editors. Ron Meyer helped me navigate the academic publishing world and eventually helped include this book in the Harriman Institute Series. I am grateful to Lindsay Martin and her OSUP team for shepherding the manuscript along with utmost professionalism. The anonymous reviewers for the press were extremely astute, and their feedback significantly helped along my own thinking.

I appreciate that Svetlana Vassileva-Karagyozova and Edith Clowes are the kind of friends and colleagues who pestered me about historical context, despite my own occasional disavowal of history. Katherine Bowers read and commented on various parts of the book. Alison Annunziata and Rebecca Pyatkevich have shared hotel rooms and many academic and nonacademic conversations about the grotesque with me. Amanda Allan was a phenomenal copyeditor whose work gave me the confidence I needed to finish the book. And I am grateful to Emma Lieber for always being a willing interlocutor and as attached to messy literary bodies as I am.

My students at the University of Kansas have heard some version or other of this book, especially in the seminar on the grotesque in spring 2013. I am grateful to them for bearing with me and for being good listeners. I was a humanities research fellow at the Hall Center for the Humanities in fall 2013, which allowed me to spend a semester on writing and research. I was also fortunate to receive a first-book subvention from the Harriman Institute at Columbia that helped defray the costs of publication.

I am grateful to my mother- and father-in-law, Meg and John, for being loving grandparents who like babysitting. My father lives far away, but I am grateful for our many phone conversations over the years and for his help and support when it was most needed. My mother and grandmother have passed on the kind of strength that only strong women can—I would not be who I am without their unconditional love and support. Most recently, I am deeply grateful to them for making their way to various Slavic events as intrepid babysitters.

My husband John has loved and believed in me for over a decade. As always, he is my rock and my best friend. These past couple of years, he spent many hours with our toddler while mommy was otherwise preoccupied with this book. It was only fitting that much of this book was written while I was pregnant with our son, Luke. Knowing and loving him has been the most miraculous thing in my life, and I think his growth in tandem with the development of this book captures the power of our bodies, a power I believe only Dostoevsky understood in its fullness.

MAKING THE FAMILIAR STRANGE

Eliminating Gentry Privilege in Russian Grotesque Realism

In a strange turn of events, Dementy Varlamovich Brudasty, omnipotent governor of Glupov (Foolsbury), suddenly appears decapitated in Mikhail Saltykov-Shchedrin's scathing allegory of Russia's past, *History of a Town* (1869–70). With no traces of actual violence, a secretary finds the governor's body "dressed in its official coat . . . seated at the desk" while his head lies in front, "completely empty," "like some flamboyant paperweight."[1] This terror-inducing, surreal moment confirms rumors that the taciturn governor, who only ever shouts a few threatening sentences to his unhappy subjects, has a music box as a head. Through the figure of the governor with his part-human and part-object hybridity, Saltykov-Shchedrin captured his disillusionment with Russia's authoritarian leaders and the arbitrariness of their leadership. Over the years, many tsars uttered their fair share of unilateral commands, while refusing to engage their subjects. But what is interesting about Saltykov-Shchedrin's approach is that rather than crafting a dictatorial figure in the realist idiom, he pushes the envelope further through stylistic exaggeration that can be characterized as *grotesque*.

---

1. Saltykov-Shchedrin, *Sobranie sochinenii*, 8:285.

A style that renders the world unreliable and strange through the "unstable mixture of heterogeneous elements,"[2] the grotesque is powerfully reflected in the monstrous image of Dementy Varlamovich Brudasty. A frightening intermingling of a human being with an inorganic object, the governor is an affront to "classificatory systems."[3] Once these categorical boundaries are breached, the hybrid creatures that emerge, as in the case of the monster in Mary Shelley's *Frankenstein,* appear capable of only the outside performance of life, a perfunctory routine stripped of higher meaning. In Saltykov-Shchedrin's mock history of Russia, this type of grotesque hybridity spreads from Glupov's tyrannical rulers to its townspeople, who similarly show no evidence of having inner lives but either are reduced to the level of objects in their slothfulness or display animalistic features by living exclusively for the gratification of physical needs.

Written a few years after Tsar Alexander II's Great Reforms (1861–74), *History of a Town* contains both historical implications and timely observations about the late 1860s. Through the endless succession of one authoritarian ruler after another, Saltykov-Shchedrin boldly critiques the country's political failings by comparing it to a mad town inhabited by mad people. Through exaggeration and caricatures, he captures Russia's perpetual history with political tyranny and calls into question the possibility that the Great Reforms could produce meaningful change.

Saltykov-Shchedrin's narrative echoes a broader sense of disappointment in Russia at the time. According to historians, beginning with the momentous 1861 emancipation of the serfs, the reforms were expected to reshape the country, but they did little to improve the lot of the peasant or any other group in Russian society. Discontent and disappointment with the country's political stagnancy spread immediately after the emancipation. Liberalism flourished, signaling a divide between the government and its people—citizens asked for fiscal and judicial reform, as well as the abolition of privilege in favor of a representative government.[4] At the same time, a more radical, "revolutionary conspiratorial tradition" also acquired a permanent foothold,[5] as "the motley variety of revolutionary types" called for the end of tsarism.[6] Around this period, in typical uncompromising fashion, the famous left-wing critic Dmitry Pisarev demanded the "successful overthrow of the reigning Romanov

---

2. Kayser, *The Grotesque in Art and Literature,* 53.

3. Harpham, *On the Grotesque: Strategies of Contradiction in Art and Literature,* 5.

4. Kornilov, *Modern Russian History,* 72–73.

5. Ulam, *In the Name of the People: Prophets and Conspirators in Prerevolutionary Russia,* 18.

6. Berlin, Hardy, and Kelly, *Russian Thinkers,* 35.

dynasty and the transformation of the political and social structure." "What is dead and rotten," wrote Pisarev, in another example of hyperbole from the period, "must of itself fall into the grave. It remains for us to give it a last push and throw the dirt over their stinking corpses."[7]

The stinking corpses of tsarist Russia in Pisarev's rhetoric and the governor with a music box for a head in Saltykov-Shchedrin's *History of a Town* are both instances of hyperbolic expression aimed at conveying an abnormal and even outright inhuman state of affairs. In this book, I focus on this national discontent and its broader hyperbolic expressions in Russian literature. Whereas Saltykov-Shchedrin's theater of the grotesque was at times fantastical to the point of inviting disbelief, the prevalent disappointment with the reforms also found more understated though still dramatic representation in several realist novels from this period. Without resorting to entirely unrealistic characters like Brudasty or other wild Glupov residents, in novels written during and after the implementation of the Great Reforms (1869–99) Fyodor Dostoevsky, Lev Tolstoy, Nikolai Leskov, Ivan Goncharov, and even Saltykov-Shchedrin himself used elements of the grotesque to convey their disenchantment with Russia and what they perceived as its spiritual shortcomings. In the novels I discuss, realism was mixed in with the grotesque and grew punchier through its rhetorical strategies, while also tempering the grotesque's more extreme caricatures. The result was an artistic lens that was neither wholly realism nor a pure grotesque but rather a composite style I term *grotesque realism*. Grotesque realism shares properties of both styles: like the grotesque, it produced a warped portrayal of the world with a focus on the body and hybrid unshapeliness, while simultaneously retaining realism's priorities by adhering to verisimilitude and never fully leaping into the supernatural. But whereas realism itself inadvertently replicated the status quo through its mimetic work, infusion with the grotesque, with its mishmash of categories, allowed the Russian novel to reflect the instability of the Great Reform and the exigencies of socioeconomic change.

This book zeroes in on grotesque realism, which, like the political phenomena of liberalism and radicalism, may be viewed as a corollary literary expression of disappointment in the Great Reforms. Historically, Russians saw themselves and their country as quintessentially soulful, whether due to their religious

---

7. Pisarev, *Sochineniia*, 125, 126.

piety or their deep emotionality.[8] Indeed, one might argue that the Russian realist novel is a canon obsessed with psychological depth. The reader will surely remember that when Raskolnikov from Dostoevsky's *Crime and Punishment* is asked about how he spends his days, he unapologetically responds that he is busy thinking. As one of many tortured thinkers who occupy the pages of Russian literature, Dostoevsky's redeemed murderer is not alone in this favored activity.

But *Russian Grotesque Realism: The Great Reforms and Gentry Decline* is not about the great thinkers of Russian literature. Instead, it is a book about the canon's nonthinkers, a no less significant group that I argue is depicted through the lens of grotesque realism. These nonthinkers are a more diffuse category with varying traits. Some of the examples I consider include characters whose lives are driven by materialism; characters who live for the physiological layer of existence; characters who do not spontaneously engage with life but blindly follow an ideology they will not or cannot break; characters whose behavior has an animalistic quality; characters whose behavior resembles that of the inhuman automaton; and, finally, characters who behave in some of these ways because they compartmentalize and shut down parts of themselves due to psychological turmoil. These figures and others like them appear throughout Russian literature alongside more overtly spiritual individuals and introduce an identity struggle through their complete absence of spiritual purpose. This spiritual erosion is particularly reflected in representations of the Russian gentry, a group once described by Karamzin as "the soul and noble image of the entire nation."[9] In late nineteenth-century realism, once the Great Reforms changed their socioeconomic and legal status, gentry characters also lost many of their spiritual values on the literary page. It is this spiritual depletion of a core demographic of the Russian novel that is at the heart of this book.

There is little consensus among historians about how the Great Reforms affected the gentry and the course of their future.[10] This book, while not

8. Berdiaev, *The Origin of Russian Communism*, 8–9. Berdyaev describes the Russian soul as comparable to the Russian steppe.

9. See Karamzin, "Priiatnye vidy, nadezhdy i zhelaniia nyneshnego vremeni," 2:275. I was directed to this quote by Bella Grigoryan, "Noble Farmers: The Provincial Landowner in the Russian Cultural Imagination," 75.

10. There are several contradicting opinions about what transpired with the Russian estate system as a result of the Great Reforms. For a sampling of different opinions, see Blum, *The End of the Old Order in Europe*; Haimson, *The Politics of Rural Russia, 1905–1914*; Freeze, "The Soslovie (Estate) Paradigm and Russian Social History," 11–36. Two particularly opposed points of view are Roberta Manning's argument about gentry decline in *The Crisis of the Old Order in Russia: Gentry and Government* and Seymour Becker's later argument about the gentry finding new avenues to succeed in *Nobility and Privilege in Late Imperial Russia*.

claiming to resolve historical questions, contributes a literary perspective to these debates. The elimination of serfdom and the reform of the courts and local government deeply affected the gentry by stripping several legislative privileges that set them apart. This historical context provides an essential backdrop to the parallel, dramatic change in literary portrayals of the group. Following the emancipation of the serfs, aside from losing legal privileges, the gentry also lost their privileged status within Russian realism, a canon devoted to their depiction. In a sense mirroring the socioeconomic disruption taking place historically in their lives, gentry characters also underwent something akin to a spiritual crisis in literature, which was conveyed by Russian writers through a broadening of realism with devices of the grotesque.

We can trace the first glimpses of the grotesque to the anti-nihilist novel, a new literary genre of the 1860s that captured the pulse of its time.[11] While thinkers of diverse social backgrounds, like Nikolai Chernyshevsky, embraced materialism as a means of equalizing all social classes through shared biology, anti-nihilist writers inverted this paradigm in their works. In response to legislature aimed at greater socioeconomic parity, Russian writers vilified a new generation of people from mixed social backgrounds. Instead of recognizing the scientific and social equality sought by the new generation, they showed the new men as inhuman and distorted their ideas. In the process, writers began a tradition of grotesque realism, which, with its inherent emphasis on classificatory confusions, became the perfect vehicle for painting moral and spiritual failures as tantamount to inhumanity.

Despite these beginnings as a derogatory idiom for social outsiders, as I show, grotesque realism was eventually redirected toward Russian realism's ultimate insiders, the gentry. The realist novel is normally understood as a middle-class institution, but in a Russian context there is no equivalent to the European middle class.[12] So instead, it was the gentry who were the most important demographic. Throughout the nineteenth century, novels blossomed around gentry heroes and heroines whose spiritual strivings engendered manifold plotlines. Although many gentry characters were spiritual seekers, this book fleshes out another side of the literary history of this group in the last three decades of the nineteenth century. For each gentry seeker of spiritual emancipation with a complex interiority there was also a sinful creature mired in animalistic fleshy passions or, worse, gentry characters

---

11. Works of grotesque realism made an appearance in the nineteenth-century after Gogol and before the period on which the book focuses, but pieces like Dostoevsky's *Village of Stepanchikovo* were too humorous to compare with the abysmal and purely negative view on reality witnessed in the late nineteenth-century grotesque.

12. Todd, "The Ruse of the Russian Novel," 404.

indifferent and detached to the point of seeming robotic or automatized. The reader may not often stumble upon individuals with music boxes for heads in the novel, but Russian grotesque realism reflects its own, more domesticated range of grotesque hybridities through characters that appear normal but whose true humanity has become eroded.

I.   THE NOBILITY AND THE GREAT REFORMS OF ALEXANDER II

Before I address how the grotesque came to shape depictions of the gentry in the Russian novel, some discussion is necessary of the historical and literary conditions that helped beget Russian grotesque realism. Late nineteenth-century Russia was defined by profound transition and the breakdown of traditional family and social structures, largely instigated by Alexander II's Great Reforms. The catalyst for these reforms was Russia's humiliating defeat at the hands of Great Britain and France in the Crimean War (1853–56). Despite not suffering great territorial losses, Russia was humbled at the Paris Treaty concluding the war, where she was no longer treated like a great power but was compelled to disarm the Black Sea coast. As Orlando Figes writes, following the Crimean War, "The image many Russians had built up of their country—the biggest, richest, and most powerful in the world—had suddenly been shattered."[13] The defeat exposed the failures of Russian infrastructure and the lack of technological advancement in both the army and navy. Afterward, there was an overwhelming cry for socioeconomic reform to redeem the country's perceived backwardness.

Largely in response to the Crimean defeat, Alexander II, though not inherently a liberal, set the Great Reforms into motion. Once called "the greatest single piece of state-directed social engineering in modern European history before the twentieth century,"[14] the 1861 Emancipation Proclamation had a powerful impact on nineteenth-century Russian society. As Daniel Field argues, the proclamation may have "emancipated very imperfectly,"[15] but the deliverance of twenty million people from bondage was a significant watershed for imperial Russia.[16] Many earlier understandings of social and eco-

---

13. Figes, *The Crimean War: A History,* 443.

14. Emmons, *The Russian Landed Gentry and the Peasant Emancipation of 1861,* 414. I was directed to this source and the quote by reading the edited volume by Eklof, Bushnell, and Zakharova, *Russia's Great Reforms, 1855–1881.*

15. Ridding the nation of serfdom did not improve the economic conditions of the Russian peasant. Peasants were given freedom but did not receive adequate lands to sustain their livelihood and remained inferior to nonpeasants.

16. Field, *The End of Serfdom: Nobility and Bureaucracy in Russia, 1855–1861,* 41.

nomic hierarchies persisted, but the egregious, arbitrary, and limitless power of landowner over serf lost its legality.[17]

Although it forged a path for the long, drawn-out process through which the peasant's lot would improve, scholars view the Emancipation and the Great Reforms that followed as more immediately significant for landowners than for peasants. One prevalent view, reflected in literary works from near the turn of the century, like Chekhov's *The Cherry Orchard* (1904), is that the reforms were "an enormous economic blow"[18] that caused "decline and disintegration"[19] for the gentry. The elimination of "serfdom as a structure" deeply affected the gentry's legal and social status while other Great Reforms further deprived them of privilege.[20] As Roberta Manning argues, landowners, who were previously accustomed to extracting revenue from estates where serfs performed agricultural labor, lacked training and practical judgment about agricultural matters.[21] When landowners were left in charge of their estates, the results were poor management, declines in revenue,[22] and an overall "prolonged period of crisis for the old political order."[23] Such an interpretation of postreform gentry life is by no means uncontested; other historians, like Seymour Becker, view the loss of serf labor as an opportunity for the gentry to reinvent themselves through alternate avenues for profit and entrepreneurship.[24]

But regardless of how one chooses to interpret the gentry's response, the emancipation and Great Reforms had an overwhelming effect on this group, significantly altering their lifestyle. The most important change initiated by the reforms related to legal privilege. Prereform Russia was a society shaped by privilege. Since Petrine times, it had been hierarchically ordered according to four traditional estates (*soslovie*)—the gentry, clergy, merchants, and peasants. Based on earlier European social models, the Russian estates were ascribed caste connotations as late as the 1860s in Vladimir Dal's Russian language dictionary.[25] At the same time, as many scholars have noted, the different estates in Russia were not as strictly separated as in the rest of Europe. The Russian estates were porous at best—divided into subgroups or sharing popu-

---

17. For a detailed account on how land was distributed during the emancipation see Kornilov, 2:45–54.

18. Manning, 8.

19. Ibid., 3.

20. Larissa Zakharova, "Autocracy and the Reforms of 1861–1874 in Russia," 34.

21. Manning, 8.

22. For a discussion of the causes of disintegration in the countryside estate, see Manning, 3–12.

23. Ibid., 3.

24. See Becker, *Nobility and Privilege in Late Imperial Russia*.

25. Freeze, 19.

lation groups with other estates. But even within this loose system, the nobility, or the first estate, possessed the most privileges. Before the 1861 reforms, the ability to own land with serfs attached to it was the basis for wealth in pre-industrial Russia and by far the gentry's most significant privilege. They were also entitled to trials by juries of their peers and exceptions from personal taxation, compulsory labor service, military conscription, and corporal punishment.

With the 1861 Emancipation, the nobility lost their most important and most valued legal privilege—serf labor. Other Great Reforms, like the 1864 establishment of the *zemstvo* or local government, the 1864 reform of the courts, the 1870 reform of city government, and others, kept chipping away at privilege by establishing legislative and juridical institutions where all estates were represented and, at least nominally, treated equitably. For instance, the judicial reform of 1864 was inspired by a belief in "the equality of all citizens before the court," irrespective of estate distinctions.[26] The extent to which estate distinctions disappeared has been a very polemical question among historians who disagree about how the Great Reforms changed the Russian estate system. Some argue that the estates gave rise to a class society in the late nineteenth century,[27] while others believe that Russia lacked proper estates with corporate rights so they could not give rise to a class system.[28] There are also historians who see late nineteenth-century Russia as defined by a messier coexistence of the older estates with a budding class system.[29] The complex historiography of the Russian estates further complicates questions about how the Great Reforms affected the gentry.

This book takes its cue from historical debates about the impact of the Great Reforms on the gentry in order to explore the status of gentry privilege within the bounds of a different sphere: the Russian realist novel. I examine the historical dilemma of what happened to the gentry once the Great Reforms stripped them of their core privileges and evaluate it through the prism of their literary representations. As I show, in addition to and even independently of what occurred historically, the Great Reforms served as an important temporal benchmark for a significant altering of the gentry's literary image. In postreform literature, we witness a distinct narrative of gentry decline, which, rather than reflecting historical realities, some historians believe permeated and influenced subsequent historical interpretations of gentry life.

---

26. Afanas'ev, "Jurors and Jury Trials in Imperial Russia, 1866–1885," 214.

27. See Blum, *The End of the Old Order in Europe*; Haimson.

28. See Confino, "The 'Soslovie' (Estate) Paradigm: Reflections on Some Open Questions," 681–99.

29. Freeze, 11–36.

II. GENTRY PRIVILEGE IN RUSSIAN REALISM

One cannot properly understand the transformation of the gentry through the grotesque without first accounting for their earlier place in Russian realism. In 1871, in the midst of the Great Reforms, Dostoevsky chastised fellow realist writers for their alienation from Russia's actualities and exclusive focus on gentry life. "It really is all gentry-landowner literature," he wrote in a letter to Nikolai Strakhov about the writings of Tolstoy and Turgenev. "It has said everything it had to say (magnificently by Lev Tolstoy). But this word, aristocratic to the higher degree, was the last. A *new word,* replacing the landowner's, still does not exist."[30] As the most famous non-gentry Russian writer, Dostoevsky was conscious of the role of privilege in Russian belles lettres. He was in a position to discern and frown upon the privilege and disproportionate attention allotted to the gentry by a group of their peers, the "landowner writers," who only understood gentry realities.

Dostoevsky declared himself uniquely qualified to offer this "new word" to the novel, no doubt intending to stake out his own territory as a realist. But no matter how self-serving or provocative, his indictment of fellow writers is also remarkably perceptive. After all, what would become of the masterpieces of Russian realism without picturesque gentry manors and lavish urban quarters, or the beloved heroes and heroines living inside these spaces? The reader of Russian realism has etched in his or her brain the manicured fingers of the middle-aged dandy Pavel Kirsanov, the lively laughter of Natasha Rostova, the housecoat of Ilya Oblomov, and many such images that arise from what Dostoevsky saw as the outmoded cocoon of gentry existence. Exceptions aside, the Russian realist novel would hardly be the same without their refined whims and emotional sensibilities. Depictions of the gentry were not universally positive, but the novel's longstanding partiality for their spiritual struggles, strivings, and failings is unabashed, almost too obvious for the critic to underscore. Dostoevsky, who believed that postreform Russia was living through "the most troubled, the most awkward, the most transitory, and the most fateful moment, perhaps, in [its] whole history," found this partiality for the gentry minority rather myopic.[31]

In the end, his challenge, whether Dostoevsky realized it or not, did not go unanswered. Prompted by the reforms and the legal loss of gentry privilege,

---

30. Dostoyevsky, *Polnoe sobranie sochinenii v tridsati tomakh,* 29.1: 216. All other references refer to this edition of references to Dostoevsky's collected works. I was directed to this quote by Joseph Frank's book *Dostoevsky: The Miraculous Years, 1865–1871,* 424. I am using Frank's translation.

31. Dostoevsky, 21:58.

or the social transitions that beset Russian society, or other, more intangible reasons, Russian realists eventually began to show a different outlook on the gentry. Fast-forwarding to 1904, when Anton Chekhov finished *The Cherry Orchard*, the gentry microcosm so pivotal in Russian realist novels was being permanently laid to rest. By the end of the play, the manor and the garden, both essential spaces for the Russian gentry, are either in shambles or completely destroyed. The owners themselves are equally decrepit; characters like Lyubov Raevskaya, who sells her estate to settle her debts, are out of touch with financial realities and spend their days in languid inactivity.

Instead of bemoaning the fall of the gentry, Chekhov shifts the focus to a different character, the merchant Lopakhin, a new hero of sorts. The son of peasants, Lopakhin builds a financial empire single-handedly. After purchasing Raevskaya's estate, he cries out, "I've bought the estate where my grandfather and my father were slaves."[32] Descended from peasant stock himself, Chekhov did not depict Lopakhin as stereotypically crass and low but wrote the role specifically for Constantine Stanislavsky, hoping that the latter's theatrical talent would forge a new merchant hero.[33]

Looking ahead to Chekhov's play as a chronological conclusion of sorts for realism, this book considers what happens to portrayals of the gentry in Russian literature in the decades between Dostoevsky's challenge and the proverbial death of the Russian gentry microcosm in *The Cherry Orchard*. Covering the period from 1869 to 1899, I argue that although the gentry remained a dominant presence in the Russian realist novel during this time, their depictions evolved significantly.

A social sphere of its own that could mirror and subvert social realities, Russian realism at first allowed the nobility to retain their privileged place in literature, even as the Great Reforms stripped them of their legal privileges. But eventually, perhaps as a prelude to Chekhov's new merchant hero, the gentry literary image grew increasingly blemished, going from ambiguous to outright negative. Even as they kept appearing and reappearing in the pages of Russian fiction, gentry characters were no longer the same in many late nineteenth-century novels. An aesthetic of psychological monstrosity, initially employed to depict social outsiders and non-gentry literary characters, was used to show the flaws of the gentry. This aesthetic, characterized by despiritualization, dehumanization, and at times ugliness, manifested key traits of the

---

32. Chekhov, *Vishnevyi sad: Komediia v chetyrikh deistviakh*, 13:240.

33. Conscious of his own merchant roots, Stanislavsky passed on the role, which led to a more conventional stage recreation of Lopakhin as an unrefined merchant. But that outcome notwithstanding, Chekhov's intention was clear. See Senderovich, "*The Cherry Orchard*: Chekhov's Last Testament," 13–14.

grotesque. With its ability to estrange the familiar without fully effacing it, the grotesque proved an adept mode for conveying changing attitudes toward the gentry.

III. REFASHIONING REALITY THROUGH THE LENS OF GROTESQUE REALISM

In coming to terms with the transformation that occurred in Russian realism between Dostoevsky's remarks and Chekhov's play, it is worth noting that realism is not always an ideal style for capturing social change. A hotly contested notion, realism has been described by Ian Watt as "a full and authentic report of human experiences [. . .] under an obligation to satisfy its reader with such details of the story as the individuality of the actors concerned, the particulars of the times and places of their actions."[34] The realist novel thus aims at verisimilitude—the reproduction of reality, or the impression of such a reproduction. Realist writers can be almost pictorial in their mimetic endeavors and seemingly reaffirm the world's existing hues and nuances. "Any honest accounting for the real, in the sense of the appearances of the world," writes Peter Brooks, "needs to give a sense of the thereness of the physical world, as in a still-life painting."[35] This sense of thereness is a fundamental reason for why realism is more likely to endorse the status quo rather than show it as fluid and changeable. As D. A. Miller argues in his Foucauldian study, *The Novel and the Police,* in their empirical mission of recreating reality's thingness, realist authors foster stability and reinvent the policing power of the law "in the very practice of novelistic representation."[36]

It is partly due to the ties between realism and the status quo that any substantial change in the literary image of the Russian gentry required that the aesthetic of realism be expanded through another lens, one more attuned to instability and social change—the grotesque. The resulting composite style, or grotesque realism, allowed Russian realist writers to transcend the imperative of empirical stability and recast reality in a new light.

On the flip side, in order to fit into the realist paradigm and render realism more radical, the grotesque had to be tempered considerably and stripped of its more outlandish components. Described as a "protean idea capable of assuming a multitude of forms," the grotesque is an inherently elusive subject

---

34. Watt, *The Rise of the English Novel,* 32.
35. Brooks, *Realist Vision,* 16.
36. Miller, *The Novel and the Police,* 20

for definition.[37] With uncertain origins and marginalized in aesthetic theory, the grotesque has been said to evolve over time, thus granting every period its unique variant. Looking through critical investigations of the grotesque for a coherent set of features, it becomes apparent that the scholarly corpus is no less protean than the style itself. "In mastering the field, one watches it atomize into fine mist," writes Geoffrey Harpham about studies of the grotesque.[38] His statement is readily corroborated in the large theoretical discrepancy between two foremost scholars writing on the grotesque, Wolfgang Kayser in *The Grotesque in Art and Literature* and Mikhail Bakhtin in *Rabelais and His World.* Kayser views the grotesque as a dark and ominous distortion, while Bakhtin believes it to be a happy and comic upturning of reality.[39]

In venturing to provide a definition, then perhaps the least polemical thing we could say about the grotesque is that its essence lies in the eye of the beholder. As virtually anyone writing about the style agrees, the grotesque effect is built upon our expectations of how things should be or appear. For instance, it is the expectation that a town have a proper governor and that such a figure possess a functioning brain that produces the grotesquery of Saltykov-Shchedrin's Brudasty. "The grotesque is the estranged world," writes Kayser.[40] Unlike the fantastic, which comes into being through the interaction of the natural with the supernatural,[41] the grotesque renders the worlds we know unreliable.

For this reason, the nature of these grotesque transformations varies depending on the text. Bakhtin, who provides an alternate definition of the grotesque as a style that inherits "the spirit of carnival," suggests that the grotesque could be construed as an estrangement from day-to-day reality that becomes friendlier and comedic, rather than dark and ominous.[42] For Bakhtin, grotesque estrangement relates to the carnival and the "peculiar logic of the 'inside out' (á l'envers), of the 'turnabout,' of a continual shifting from top to bottom, from front to rear, of numerous parodies and travesties, humiliations, profanations, comic crownings and uncrownings."[43] Bakhtin's carnival grotesque deposes authority and inverts all hierarchies, profaning the sacrosanct through laughter.

---

37. Harpham, xxi.
38. Ibid., xvii–xviii.
39. See Kayser, 184; Bakhtin, *Rabelais and His World,* 47.
40. Kayser, 184.
41. Todorov, *The Fantastic: A Structural Approach to a Literary Genre,* 20–40.
42. Bakhtin, *Rabelais and His World,* 47.
43. Ibid., 11.

As Russian society underwent a transition during the Great Reforms that estranged reality without transforming it into something completely foreign and unrecognizable, the grotesque became especially suitable as a lens for capturing this intermediary state of affairs. Scholars like Kevin Platt have already discussed with interesting results the introduction of the style in Russian literature to capture such transitory historical periods.[44] Although one might construe the reforms as ultimately a positive development, in the Russian canon this estrangement, which sometimes involved the upending of reality, did not assume the happy and comic turn that Bakhtin ascribes to the grotesque. With few notable exceptions, the grotesque estrangement of reality almost always produced a darker vision of the world.

Along these lines, an important way in which the grotesque can estrange the familiar is through seemingly unnatural and inharmonious physicality, in the form of hybridity or the conflation of categories. The paintings found underneath the Baths of Titus in Renaissance Italy (1480), which bequeathed the style its name, exemplify unnatural mixing by showcasing hybrid creatures—human and animal forms emerging from plant stems. Victor Hugo similarly underscores this hybridity in his "Preface to Cromwell," where he argues that the grotesque creates "myriads of intermediary creatures" and "impels the ghastly antics of the witches' revels [. . . it] gives Satan his horns, his cloven foot and his bat's wings."[45] The grotesque violation of boundaries thus breeds monstrosity, "misshapen, ugly, exaggerated, or even formless" images and characters,[46] monsters from the point of view of "'classic' aesthetics."[47]

If it is through such freakish others that the grotesque disrupts the world's normativity, then some adjustment is necessary when the style permeates realism, giving rise to grotesque realism. Within the bounds of realism, the deformity of the grotesque cannot manifest itself as obviously as in the person of Satan or in the frescoes underneath the Baths of Titus. Kayser, who associates the grotesque primarily with romanticism and modernism, argues that when realism flourished, the grotesque lost some of its prominence.[48] With its empirical bent, the realist novel is not very accommodating to the deliberately nonrealistic contortions of the grotesque—freakish others must technically be standard humans. Instead of overt monstrosity and violations of natural boundaries, in realism we find the *appearance* of monstrosity. The Russian

---

44. See Platt, *History in a Grotesque Key: Russian Literature and the Idea of Revolution.*
45. Elliott, ed., *The Harvard Classics,* 39:39.
46. Harpham, 5.
47. Bakhtin, *Rabelais,* 25.
48. Kayser, 104.

realist grotesque is flattened of its supernatural components and either is redirected inward into a monstrous or vacuous psyche or assumes other quieter, metaphorical tones.

The more pervasive features of estrangement in grotesque realism revolve around the category of humanity and the ways in which a human being can become dehumanized even while categorically retaining his or her biological humanity. The most important way in which authors call into question the humanity of characters is by orienting the focus externally by stripping human life of its spiritual content. This despiritualization takes different forms—some characters seem soulless because they focus all their energies on primal needs and desires like food and sex, whereas others live their lives in a seemingly unfeeling and automatized fashion. Bakhtin describes this absence or scarcity of spirit as grotesque "degradation" or "the lowering of all that is high, spiritual, ideal, abstract."[49] To characterize the style by its extremes, we might say that at one pole of the realist grotesque stands the Rabelaisian reveler, with his laughter reduced,[50] consumed by bodily longings, while at the other end appears Olympia, the automaton from E. T. A. Hoffman's "The Sandman" who is the essential human object, navigating the world mindlessly. For different reasons, neither character invests much energy into spiritual activity. Their lives progress externally as their psychic malaise assumes the shape of diminished or nearly effaced interiority.

Moving past these extremes that do not appear in realism in their full form, we can argue that the grotesque characters occupying the pages of the Russian novel realism generally fall under three broad categories of hybridity—those between the man and animal, man and corpse, and man and object. Within the context of realism these three fusions of the human with the inhuman emerge subtly, as first nihilist and then gentry characters display some element of hybridity on either a psychological or physiological level.

Looked at from the outside, the protagonists of grotesque realism are not noticeably strange; they are not supernatural monsters or other unfathomable creatures, like the governor with a music box for a head. Grotesque realism is primarily a disorder of the human soul, and its categorical confusions arise from the psychic disruption apparent in a largely externalized existence anchored on the body and its needs and processes. Similarly, grotesque realism never transcends the confines of the human body, which proves capacious

---

49. Bakhtin, *Rabelais*, 19.

50. In his Dostoevsky book, Bakhtin argues, "In carnivalized literature of the eighteenth and nineteenth centuries, laughter is as a rule considerably muffled." Bakhtin traces this "reduced laughter" in Dostoevsky's oeuvre through the Menippea. See Bakhtin, *Problems of Dostoevsky's Poetics*, 165.

enough to reflect many spiritual aberrations. To match the spiritual void, the body is subjected to purely natural distortions or disguises: a devil's costume[51] rather than an actual devil, a human face that hides demonic forces, an oddly shaped or distended body part, a body with a yellow and corpselike appearance, a body misshapen and resembling an animal, and other such examples. Grotesque realism creates human hybrids that are either animalistic or lifeless to the point of resembling an object. The human corpse, an entity no longer in control of itself and spilling foul substances and odor from every orifice, is especially fitting as a subject for the grotesque. Many of the works of grotesque realism discussed in this book feature corpses in one capacity or another.

The grotesque thus adjusts to the lens of realism, but its estrangement, hybridity, and, at times, ugliness also unlock new artistic possibilities for realism. Transferred to the psychological level, the grotesque helped render the social instability of the era of the Great Reforms. As the nihilist social newcomers introduced their materialistic worldview into the public sphere, tensions arose about the very nature of the subject—whether someone's essence was derived from their body and material conditions or from their spiritual side. At this time, the grotesque becomes helpful shorthand for Russian realist writers, who relied on its peculiar aesthetic to capture the country's difficult entry into industrialized modernity. Gentry subjects who had populated the pages of the novel from its inception became the figures through which this transition was measured, as the grotesque marked their decline during and after the Great Reforms. A desperate need for spiritual salvation and reconciliation was reflected through characters moving about the pages of Russian fiction like hollow marionettes, having succumbed to the will of others; or through gentry characters that appear like animalistic, sex-obsessed beings that objectify others, viewing them like animals or things to be used and discarded.

IV. RUSSIAN GROTESQUE REALISM, 1869–99

Not entirely unique as a Russian literary phenomenon, postreform grotesque realism relates to an earlier and purer manifestation of the grotesque penned by Gogol. It was in Gogol's *Dead Souls* (1842), often described as the "apotheosis of the grotesque,"[52] that the Russian landowner first emerged as a monstrous

---

51. An individual wearing a devil's costume that scares the town appears in Leskov's *Cathedral Folk*.

52. Fanger, *Dostoevsky and Romantic Realism: A Study of Dostoevsky in Relation to Balzac, Dickens, and Gogol*, 101.

other in Russian fiction. The Gogolian grotesque presented life "exposed in all its nakedness" and "frightful disintegration," thus serving as the epitome of the "merciless frankness" Vissarion Belinsky demanded from art at the time.[53] One might think of the landowner Sobakevich as a hybrid between man and animal, whereas Plyushkin is a cross between a human being and an object. Hard as he tried in part 2 of *Dead Souls,* Gogol could not transcend the negative, grotesque world he created. His aspirations were realized by other Russian writers like Ivan Turgenev, whose *A Sportsman's Sketches* (1852) overcame the Gogolian grotesque and bolstered the status quo through a realism capable of discerning beauty even in a world plagued by serfdom.[54]

This attitude toward reality changed during the Great Reforms when many realist writers were once again drawn to the negative grotesque gaze pioneered by Gogol. *Russian Grotesque Realism* traces the evolution of the Russian realist novel in the late nineteenth century, focusing on the role of the grotesque in that evolution. I consider attitudes toward Russian reality in seven realist novels and address how certain social groups are depicted, with a particular emphasis on the gentry. The focus on this demographic and the realist novel inform the choice of material represented in this book. It is for this reason that, for instance, I do not directly address Saltykov-Shchedrin's *History of a Town,* which falls outside the novelistic tradition, but instead concentrate on his novel *The Golovlev Family.* Although the grotesque does not reveal the same characteristics in all the works I consider, I trace a general move from a lesser to a more widespread grotesque realism. I begin with the grotesque as a style for rendering social outsiders (*The Precipice* and *Cathedral Folk*), continue with its appearance in depictions of the gentry hero (*Demons*) and heroine (*Anna Karenina*), proceed to the grotesque microcosm (*The Golovlev Family* and *Resurrection*), and conclude with the redemption of the grotesque (*The Brothers Karamazov*).

My argument is split into six chapters that collectively demonstrate how late realist writers use the grotesque to capture or, as some historians would argue, *create* the myth of gentry demise during and after the Russian Great Reforms. I trace the beginnings of the grotesque and its reintroduction into realism after Gogol, its expansion and fruition within the realist novel, and, finally, its redemption. Gogol brought a dark vision of spiritual decline into Russian literature as well as a haunting question about where Russia was heading. And just as he could not conjure a positive vision through part 2 of *Dead Souls,* so Russian realists fell short of this vision for decades. In many ways,

---

53. Quoted in Jackson, *Dialogues with Dostoevsky: The Overwhelming Questions,* 192.

54. Jackson, *Dialogues,* 200.

Dostoevsky's *The Brothers Karamazov*, with its closing moment of togetherness and celebration, may be the closest we get to redeeming the Gogolian vision of Russia and the Russian gentry.

This darker Gogolian gaze reappeared in Russian literature beginning with the anti-nihilist novels that appeared during the 1860s.[55] The first hints of the grotesque emerged in depictions of the new men of the 1860s, or "nihilists" after Turgenev's Bazarov, men who came from mixed social backgrounds and were usually members of the *raznochintsy*—a label with little legal significance other than demarcating outsider status.[56] Nihilists came to define the Russian 1860s, permeating realism and inspiring a new novelistic genre, the anti-nihilist novel, which frequently demonized nihilists by using their own language of materialism. In chapter 1, I analyze two novels with anti-nihilist features, *The Precipice* (1969) by Ivan Goncharov and *Cathedral Folk* (1872) by Nikolai Leskov, in order to show how portrayals of nihilists were colored by materialist language that paved the way for realism's new grotesque aesthetics. Rendered as monstrous, part animal and part human, nihilists evoke the grotesque both in their appearance and in their scientific and materialistic outlooks that lead them to degrade others, especially women, to the level of half-human and half-object hybrids. Gentry characters are also captured in these novels but, by and large, are lionized as positive traditional figures and foils for the grotesque nihilist. In this sense, then, while the Great Reforms worked toward instituting social change in Russian society by minimizing legal divisions, anti-nihilist writers espoused a traditional message that reinforced the estate system with the gentry on top.

While the frequently slapdash anti-nihilist novel did not achieve full-blown grotesque realism, it served as an artistic laboratory for the style's evolution. The grotesque is often associated with short stories and shorter genres that can sustain its effects.[57] For this reason, we often see primarily snapshots of the grotesque in the realist novel. In time, however, grotesque realism also expands in scope, maturing as all the while it infiltrates more mainstream works of Russian literature. The investigation of this expansion leads me into chapter 2, which explores Dostoevsky's nominally anti-nihilist novel, *Demons* (1872), a work where the anti-nihilist grotesque is perpetuated through hybrid

---

55. Works of grotesque realism made an appearance in the nineteenth century after Gogol and before the period on which the book focuses, but pieces like Dostoevsky's *Village of Stepanchikovo* were too humorous to compare with the abysmal and purely negative view on reality witnessed in the late nineteenth-century grotesque.

56. See the study by Wirtschafter, *Structures of Society: Imperial Russia's "People of Various Ranks."*

57. Meindl, *American Fiction and the Metaphysics of the Grotesque, 7.*

and monstrous nihilist figures but is also reinvented as nihilists transform from freaks of the margins into powerful adversaries in charge of the social milieu. The nihilists and their sphere of activity are no longer marginalized, so the scope of the grotesque expands from the isolated person or persons to a larger grotesque microcosm. If anti-nihilist writers facilitated the beginnings of grotesque realism, as the second chapter of *Russian Grotesque Realism* reveals, the style truly blossomed and assumed its distinct characteristics in Dostoevsky's hands.

The analysis of *Demons* serves as an important point of transition in *Russian Grotesque Realism*. Introduced as a tool for the demonization of social outsiders, grotesque realism is eventually redirected, targeting traditional social groups and the gentry in particular. In *Demons* the grotesque aesthetic first extends to members of the gentry, like Nikolai Stavrogin, who fail to live up to the high expectations for their estate. Instead of serving as a leader in the community who might bring people together, Stavrogin dies by his own hand, alone in an attic. This change in the grotesque takes up the remaining four chapters of this book, which illustrate how grotesque realism becomes the aesthetic of choice for capturing the gentry decline and questions of social transition in postreform Russia.

In chapter 3, I consider Tolstoy's *Anna Karenina* (1878), where the grotesque transitions from the depiction of the gentry hero to the depiction of the gentry heroine, the passion-absorbed Anna Karenina. Anna's awakened sexuality becomes the basis for her increasingly enhanced beauty in the novel—an artful and disharmonious beauty rooted in the unnaturalness of birth control and morphine. In the course of reading the novel, one gets the sense that the more beautiful Anna becomes, the closer she comes to being an essential grotesque object, the embodiment of her own portrait. Anna's dehumanization is echoed by the grotesque dehumanization of other gentry characters in the novel, as Tolstoy shows the life of the body as equivalent to spiritual isolation. In contrast, living for the soul transcends egoism and flows out toward communal ties. These ties are particularly relevant in the postreform world of the novel, where traditional bonds face dissolution.

Chapters 4 and 5 show the expansion of the grotesque through an analysis of *The Golovlev Family* (1875–80) by Saltykov-Shchedrin and Tolstoy's later novel, *Resurrection* (1899). In chapter 4 I address the expansion and maturation of Russian grotesque realism in *The Golovlev Family*. In this novel, Saltykov-Shchedrin captures the degradation of the Russian gentry family and their eventual transformation into animal-like monsters due to an inability to function in the new, postreform world. Aware of a literary tradition that focused on the gentry family, Saltykov-Shchedrin upturns earlier paradigms by constructing grotesque doubles of landowner protagonists like the Bagrovs from Sergei Aksakov's *Family Chronicle* (1856). In the twenty years between Aksakov's chronicle and Saltykov-Shchedrin's novel, the image of the gentry was significantly altered and tarnished. Hollow beings devoid of spirituality, singularly preoccupied with food and other bodily pleasures, Saltykov-Shchedrin's Golovlev landowners are hardly human and hardly alive—they emerge as part-animal and part-corpse hybrids.

Even more so than *Anna Karenina*, Tolstoy's *Resurrection*, the last Russian realist novel of the nineteenth century and the subject of chapter 5, casts a dark shadow over the gentry, overturning earlier depictions of their life. By the time Tolstoy's *Resurrection* is released, the previously marginalized grotesque overtakes the aesthetic portrayal of virtually the whole of Russian reality—the grotesque person and grotesque microcosm expand into a grotesque world. If Saltykov-Shchedrin's gentry characters appear as gluttonous, hollow shells, Tolstoy's gentry are dehumanized as well, but instead of worshipping food, they are more fixated on sex and bodily pleasure. Many belong to a world no different from the milieu frequented by Tolstoy's earlier characters, but many commendable gentry figures in *War and Peace* turn into grotesque monsters in *Resurrection*.

In chapter 6 I intentionally break with chronology to conclude on the more redemptive treatment of the grotesque in Dostoevsky's *The Brothers Karamazov* (1880). Grotesque realism, which figures in descriptions of the gentry and social hybrids like the bastard Smerdyakov, emerges in all its dehumanizing power in the novel. For instance, the landowner Fyodor Karamazov literally embodies the poetics of ugliness and sexual desire that the grotesque brings into Russian realism. The struggle between corporality and spirituality, essential to the mission of the grotesque as a style and philosophical worldview, is reflected throughout *The Brothers Karamazov* in important debates about the body, sexuality, and identity among the Karamazov brothers who inherit their father's boundless sensuality. The idea of active love as preached by Father Zosima and practiced by Alyosha becomes an important force for battling the self-destructive Karamazov passions. The gaze of this active love, which deems everything human as ultimately beautiful and lovable, counters the dehumanization of the grotesque. The ending of *The Brothers Karamazov*, with Alyosha's speech at the stone as the boys are collectively going to eat pancakes, showcases the potential for redemption and reconciliation: not only can the grotesque be rehumanized through spiritual love and empathy, but Dostoevsky suggests, as Bakhtin does in his Rabelais book, that communal spiritual regeneration and harmony can be achieved through the body. This more positive portrayal of the body and the grotesque is a fitting ending to this book.

Russian Grotesque Realism fleshes out the evolution of the realist novel in late nineteenth-century Russia, providing new perspectives on the trials and tribulations of individual gentry characters through a broad survey of the Russian novel. The Russian gentry had been essential protagonists in Russian literature going back to Pushkin's days and beyond. For the most part, it was the diffidence, awkwardness, and failure of many gentry characters stemming from overactive minds that provided for the deep humanity underlying many of their portrayals. However, as the emergence of grotesque realism indicates, during the last three decades of the nineteenth century, gentry spirituality significantly waned. One of the first late nineteenth-century Russian literature characters to turn distorted and grotesque, Nikolai Stavrogin serves as an empty center where once there had been meaning and emotional and spiritual depth. Other gentry characters, like Stepan and Yudushka Golovlev, are similarly pale and distorted versions of what gentry heroes had been. They are inscrutable and empty and often seem irredeemable.

In a country as known for its "contradictions" as Russia,[58] this crisis of the soul and the grotesque debasement of the best and brightest are approached from two opposing and equally powerful perspectives. The first and earlier of these impulses, embodied in novels like *Anna Karenina* and especially *The Brothers Karamazov,* centered on love and reconciliation. Even while seeing the grotesque, Tolstoy and Dostoevsky presented grotesque individuals as marked by a failure of love. The presence of individuals who appear like grotesque caricatures, however tempting it might be to deny them fellow feeling, presented an opportunity for love and its power to redeem and humanize. In embracing the grotesque and the empty space where there once was a soul, one could reach the human within the monster and redeem it through absolute love.

On the other hand, there were irredeemably grotesque individuals in novels like *The Golovlev Family* and *Resurrection,* where the despair and hopelessness evoked was in keeping with the pessimism of the fin de siècle.[59] Although this book concludes, not unintentionally, on a positive note with *The Brothers Karamazov,* which does something radically different with the grotesque, if we follow the literary chronology directly, the phenomenon of grotesque realism obviously ends on a low note of hopelessness. Tolstoy's 1899 *Resurrection,*

---

58. Berdiaev, 18.

59. See Bowers and Kokobobo, "Introduction: The Fin-de-siècle Mood in Russian Literature," 1–14.

the last realist novel of the nineteenth century, spells the death of a particular iteration of the novel genre in Russia, and I would suggest that the dark gaze of grotesque realism may have had something to do with that. For whether the gentry underwent a parallel socioeconomic demise historically or not, the late nineteenth century was certainly a time for their demise in literature. With its former heroes displaced by dehumanized monsters, it is clear that the Russian novel as an institution for gentry spiritual strivings had come to its natural end.

CHAPTER 1

THE NIHILIST AS GROTESQUE OTHER IN IVAN GONCHAROV'S *THE PRECIPICE* AND NIKOLAI LESKOV'S *CATHEDRAL FOLK*

The label *nihilist,* which implies belief in nothing, was quite a misnomer when applied to a group of people who "believed blindly and violently in their own ideas."[1] For former seminarians, such as Nikolai Chernyshevsky and Nikolai Dobrolyubov, and implicitly for other young men of the 1860s, materialism "turned into a peculiar sort of dogmatic theology" and science became an "object of faith."[2] The new men of the 1860s loathed the status quo in imperial Russia and had little confidence in the willingness or ability of the tsarist autocracy to redeem the system from above. Instead, they were determined to expose the failures of Russian society themselves, with science and positivism as their primary tools. Much of their negative rhetoric was geared toward showing that nothingness, or *nihil,* was inherent not to them but to society itself, which they believed to be hollowed out of its intellectual energy and values. By no means reserved in their disapproval, the new men publicly expressed their distaste for contemporary Russia through social criticism in thick journals, such as *Sovremenik* and *Russkoe slovo,* and in literary works, like Chernyshevsky's *What Is to Be Done?*

---

1. Venturi, *Roots of Revolution: A History of the Populist and Socialist Movements in Nineteenth-Century Russia,* 326.

2. Berdiaev, 46.

The new men were so influential in 1860s tsarist Russia that this period is sometimes described as a "nihilist milieu" in their honor.[3] Their writings inspired journalistic and literary responses from more conservative-minded writers of fiction on the pages of the anti-nihilist novel, a genre that emerged as a "socio-cultural manifestation of Russian life"[4] on the eve of the emancipation. Key representatives of this new subgenre of the novel included works like Pisemsky's *The Troubled Sea* (1863); Leskov's *No Way Out* (1864), *At Daggers Drawn* (1872), and *Cathedral Folk* (1872); Goncharov's *The Precipice* (1869); Dostoevsky's *Demons* (1872); and others. In many of these writings, nihilists are disparaged and demonized so much that at times they appear outright inhuman. Similar aesthetic moments exist in several of these works, but in the interest of space and time, I concentrate on two of the most relevant examples, Goncharov's *The Precipice* and Leskov's *Cathedral Folk*. As I suggest, first in *The Precipice* and more prominently in *Cathedral Folk*, the nihilist is described as a monstrous other through the aesthetic of grotesque realism. The style was still in its infancy at this stage and not nearly as developed as in the later 1870s, but its first stirrings in the anti-nihilist novel influenced future manifestations.

Scholars have already suggested that although technically part of the realist canon, anti-nihilist novels departed from the empirical objectivity of realism in their excessively critical portrayals of nihilists. In keeping with the anti-nihilist bias, Russian writers captured the ideology of the new men in a simplistic and exaggerated fashion, often demeaning the nihilists themselves as bearers of pernicious new ideas. As Serge Gregory argues, not only did portrayals of nihilists in such novels lack psychological depth, but nihilists were outright dehumanized; they were rendered as abnormal, base "mutants and reptiles."[5] Similarly, in an article about Leskov's lengthy and aesthetically inferior anti-nihilist novel, *At Daggers Drawn*, Ilya Vinitsky cites various fantastic occurrences, such as visions, secret voices, moving objects, and other such moments. As he posits, Leskov may have been attempting to counter the rationalism of the new men with its opposite social phenomenon, a belief in the supernatural.[6]

Although Goncharov and Leskov adhere to the basic empirical expectations of realism in *The Precipice* and *Cathedral Folk* and refrain from turning nihilist characters into literal "mutants" or "reptiles," they nonetheless engage

3. See the first three chapters of Moser, *Antinihilism of the Russian Novel of the 1860s*.

4. Starygina, *Russkii roman v situatsii filosofsko-religioznoi polemiki 1860–1870-kh godov*, 11.

5. Gregory, "Dostoevsky's *The Devils* and the Antinihilist Novel," 447.

6. See Vinitsky, "Russkie dukhi—spiritualisticheskii siuzhet romana N. S. Leskova 'Na nozhakh' v ideologicheskom kontekste 1860-kh godov," accessed online on 10/14/15 at http://magazines.russ.ru/nlo/2007/87/vi10.html.

in hyperbolic expression by encoding these characters with a subtler hybridity. Their disparaging portrayals of nihilists bear important traits of grotesque realism by reflecting the coexistence of psychological and sometimes physiological qualities from both man and animal. In many respects, nihilists invited this grotesque aesthetic through both their social backgrounds and their ideological beliefs. Their mixed heritage as members of the *raznochintsy* was compatible with the hybridity of the grotesque. On the other hand, their devotion to science and espousal of materialism fit well with the style's aesthetics and its degradation of highbrow idealism to the level of body and matter.

Indeed, what I would argue is that in their use of the grotesque in portrayals of nihilist characters like Mark Volokhov (*The Precipice*), Varnava Prepotensky (*Cathedral Folk*), and Izmail Termosesov (*Cathedral Folk*), Goncharov and Leskov engaged the materialism of the new generation, recreating its core tenets, such as Chernyshevsky's view of man as yet another animal. But whereas Chernyshevsky presented his materialist views in a straightforward manner, anti-nihilist writers like Goncharov and Leskov exaggerated such ideas through their grotesque aesthetic. In *The Precipice* and *Cathedral Folk* the grotesque assumed a two-layered aesthetic form and was used to stylize both the nihilists and their victims. Anti-nihilist writers used hybridity to lower nihilists characters to the level of grotesque bodies, while simultaneously showing how these characters dehumanized others and viewed the world as a grotesque theater. In a reality threatened by nihilists and their grotesque materialism, the gentry came forward as bearers of traditional values and as society's keepers; in face of the nihilist threat, the country's salvation lay in their hands.

I.   THE MATERIALIST PREROGATIVE: CHERNYSHEVSKY AND THE IDEOLOGY OF THE GROTESQUE

On the level of representation, the grotesque might be said to shift the essence of personality from mind to body. Bakhtin, who most directly engages the body as a fundamental component of the grotesque, views physical processes and corpulence as what distinguish the aesthetic lens of the grotesque. In *Rabelais and His World* he discusses the appearance of the body in the grotesque and the process by which this style degrades, "turn[ing] [its] subject into flesh."[7] To illustrate this degradation, Bakhtin cites several examples from the Middle Ages during which learned discourse is "often debased to the

---

7. Bakhtin, *Rabelais*, 20.

bodily level of food, drink, digestion, and sexual life."[8] This discursive debasement of higher ideals was also relevant in writings by nineteenth-century left-wing critics whose materialist lens paralleled the degradation prevalent in the grotesque. Indeed, the grotesque's focus on physicality at the expense of the spirit may be one reason for why the style made a comeback on the Russian literary scene during the 1860s.

The new generation's materialism was rooted in key concepts formulated by Chernyshevsky, often perceived as the leader of the nihilist movement. Western critics have questioned the systematicity of Chernyshevsky's materialism, deeming it simplistic and a form of "materialistic biologism."[9] In contrast, Soviet scholars have traditionally seen Chernyshevsky as an exceptional materialist thinker, second only to Marx. Irrespective of his imperfections as writer and thinker, Chernyshevsky and other men of the 1860s were considerably more invested in materialism and material realities than the previous generation of idealists.

The "clearest, most publicly resonant statement" of Chernyshevsky's materialism can be encountered in "The Anthropological Principle in Philosophy" (1860).[10] In this work, influenced by Feuerbach and Buchner as well as newer lights of materialism like Moleschott, Emil du Bois-Reymond, and Karl Vogt,[11] Chernyshevsky opposes traditional perceptions of human beings as a duality between body and spirit. As Irina Paperno argues, through Feuerbach and his idea of the "essential inseparability of spirit and matter," Chernyshevsky found a way to reconcile "the romantic oppositions of ideal and real, soul and body."[12] Like Feuerbach, Chernyshevsky focuses on man's material nature, which he sees as the basis for the subject outside all philosophies and religious ideals. Putting aside all "psychological and moral-philosophical problems," he suggests that he would like to see man merely "as a being that possesses a stomach, a head, bones, muscles and nerves."[13]

This radical lowering of the individual to essentially the level of an object—a being with a stomach and bones—evokes a philosophical perspective similar to that motivating the grotesque. Although Chernyshevsky's philosophy does not preclude the subject from having a soul,[14] it diverts attention

---

8. Ibid.

9. Zenkovsky, *A History of Russian Philosophy*, 1:329.

10. Clowes, *Fiction's Overcoat: Russian Literary Culture and the Question of Philosophy*, 78.

11. Scanlan, "Nicholas Chernyshevsky and Philosophical Materialism in Russia," 69.

12. Paperno, *Chernyshevsky and the Age of Realism: A Study in the Semiotics of Behavior*, 65–66.

13. Chernyshevsky, 268.

14. And, as it has been argued, due to censorship he could not do so in the press (Scanlan, 73–74).

away from the soul, focusing on the subject's physical makeup. What matters in Chernyshevsky's thought are the bones, muscles, and nerves that constitute the subject and render him or her susceptible to the physical properties of objective reality. These objective realities determine psychology rather than the other way around. The individual is thus lowered to the level of bodily appendages, a degradation paralleled in anti-nihilist novels where Chernyshevsky's philosophical ideas assume theoretical and poetic expression through the representation of nihilists as grotesque hybrids.

Another important link between Chernyshevsky's ideas and the anti-nihilist novel can be found in the way both writings approach the relationship between human beings and animals. As Chernyshevsky argues, humans are ultimately no different from animals and plants in their susceptibility to the same laws of nature.[15] He illustrates this likeness through some radical comparisons. For instance, he presents a similarity between the "process that takes place in Newton's nervous system in discovering the law of gravity and that process that takes place in the nervous system of the fowl that finds an oat grain in a dung heap."[16] Although Chernyshevsky qualifies this outlandish comparison, this view of man as yet another animal is prominent in "The Anthropological Principle in Philosophy."

Chernyshevsky goes so far as to claim that animals are not inferior to humans even when it comes to higher processes such as reasoning or consciousness. In a comparison between humans and dogs, he contends that the two are no different and that the dog possesses the same basic psychic capabilities as the human being. The dog, according to Chernyshevsky, is more than capable of complex thinking processes: "You raise a stick to a dog; the dog runs away with its tail between its legs. . . . It did indeed act by instinct and mechanically, but not entirely; out of instinctual habit, it mechanically put its tail between its legs when it ran away from you, but conscious thought induced it to run."[17] This statement links together man and animal as beings that both originate from the natural world. The dog is motivated to run away from the stick by the same psychological processes that compel a man to walk away from a fellow man.

By establishing commonality between man and either inanimate objects or animals, Chernyshevsky indirectly helps construct two different types of hybridity. His fusions of frames of references through paradoxical comparisons between Newton and the brain of a fowl, or a dog running from the stick and a scared man, not only foreground the virtues of the animal but also intro-

15. Scanlan, 74.
16. Chernyshevsky, 278.
17. Ibid., 181.

duce a state of subhumanity for persons. Indeed, Chernyshevsky's matter-of-fact comparisons, which simultaneously emancipate animals and degrade the human subject, migrate to the anti-nihilist novel where they are transformed into vehement affronts. In anti-nihilist novels, the link between man and animal is reflected in the unusual figure of the nihilist. At the hands of more traditional writers, nihilists appear like intermediary, grotesque creatures that display hints of animalism in either their behaviors or their appearance.[18]

II. GONCHAROV'S MARK VOLOKHOV AS GROTESQUE HYBRID

Chernyshevsky's association of human beings with other animals in "On the Anthropological Principle in Philosophy" marks an important integration of materialism into thinking about the human subject, which is significantly represented in Goncharov's *The Precipice* (1869) and Leskov's *Cathedral Folk* (1872). These novels do not embrace grotesque realism to the point that the style envelops their entire aesthetic worlds but rather anchor any manifestations of the grotesque on nihilists and their victims. Over time, we see the grotesque expand beyond a limited person or persons, creating a grotesque aura over a space or a society. But in the anti-nihilist novel the scope of the style was still quite narrow—the style colors the representation of nihilists who appear as a cross between man and beast while also informing how nihilists construe their purported victims.

Let us first consider grotesque realism as it appears in Goncharov's *The Precipice*, which predates *Cathedral Folk*. With a long and complicated creative history, *The Precipice* was conceived during the 1840s with a cast of characters situated in the 1830s, an era of idealism. Since the writing dragged on for several decades, the novel's makeup slowly shifted as a result of significant historical events, such as the emancipation of the serfs and the Great Reforms. The novel expanded to account for these watersheds in the life of tsarist Russia, and the character of Mark Volokhov, a nihilist and man of the 1860s, was retroactively transplanted into the earlier era.

Mark's later ideological origins and his belated inclusion into the narrative virtually guaranteed his outsider status. His ideas further confirmed this

---

18. This view, though not immediately indebted to Darwinism, shared in at least part of its philosophical perception of the world as scientifically and biologically driven. Though Chernyshevsky had his other influences, nihilists like Pisarev embraced Darwinism as a life philosophy that provided explanations for human nature outside the essentialized Christian or metaphysical ones. See Vucinich, *Darwin in Russian Thought*.

status. Instead of sharing the idealism of the other male protagonist, Raisky, Volokhov possesses a worldview shaped by purely materialistic and utilitarian concerns. Much like Chernyshevsky who dramatically drew comparisons between men and dogs, Mark Volokhov views human life in strictly materialist terms as no different from animal existence. As Vera tells us following their tumultuous affair, Mark does not believe people to be capable of higher, non-utilitarian feelings. Rather, "In the name of his truth, he had dethroned man and reduced him to the level of an animal, depriving him of his other, non-animal side."[19] In this zoological model, life in human society is compared to the existence of a group of gnats crowded "in hot weather in an enormous column, colliding, moving about in a frenzy, multiplying, feeding themselves, warming themselves."[20] Depriving individuals of the possibility of altruism or deeper feelings, Mark also denies them morally inspired actions, suggesting that humans can only act on impulse to fulfill basic biological needs.

Mark's materialist and utilitarian worldview renders life in society equivalent to life in the wilderness. This kind of materialism is familiar in Russian literature going as far back as Turgenev's Bazarov. But Mark's positions seem extreme even by these standards. And as Mark degrades the world around him, Goncharov exercises his authorial privilege to turn the tables and extend this grotesque worldview to Mark himself. In this sense, Mark's materialism becomes the basis for the first hints of grotesque realism in *The Precipice*. While Mark may see others as grotesque beings deprived of higher sentiments, Goncharov invites us to view Mark in this manner. Mark does not embody the unsightliness of the grotesque in his appearance, but there is a certain hybridity about him constructed through his animalistic mannerisms, highly stylized by Goncharov.

Even before the character is introduced to readers, Raisky already hears that Mark, who is under police surveillance in the country, is a monster that treats books with disrespect and often damages them. "This Volokhov is the monster [*chudo*] of our town," exhorts Leonty Kozlov.[21] His statement calls attention to Goncharov's aesthetic stigmatization of Mark as the town's monstrous outsider. Similar clues arise from the animal roots of Mark's last name, Volokhov, which means *wolf*.

This initial classification of Mark as a part-monster and part-animal outsider is reinforced in the reader's first encounter with the character. Mark enters a room through a window, wearing trousers soiled up to his waist, after attempting to cross the Volga on a fisherman's boat. Unconcerned with

---

19. Goncharov, *Polnoe sobranie sochinenii v 20-ti tomakh*, 7:659.
20. Ibid., 7:660.
21. Ibid., 7:124.

propriety, he simply walks into Leonty's home through the window, demands food, and grabs a change of clothing from his host's wardrobe. At other times, he can be seen stealing apples from Raisky's garden with no concern for private property. These seemingly uncivilized behaviors, and Mark's general lack of respect for societal convention, help foreground the character's implicitly animalistic nature. Mark's face, which is irregular in its features, further supports this impression. The narrator describes Mark's "protruding forehead" and brown hair that resembles a horse's thick mane.[22] When finally sitting, Mark assumes an animal-like pose:

> This immobility concealed the vigilance, sensitivity, and alarm that one sometimes notices in a dog that is apparently lying calmly and without a care. Its paws pressed together, its sleeping mug rests on its paws, its spine is curled into a heavy lazy ring. The dog is completely asleep; only a single eyelid keeps trembling, the black eye beneath just barely visible. But if someone nearby were to stir, if a gust were to blow, a door to slam, a stranger to appear—all those members, arranged in a carefree way, would instantly tense, the whole figure would be fired up, emboldened, would bark, jump up.[23]

Virtually echoing Chernyshevsky's materialistic comparison of man to the dog, Goncharov shows Mark reacting to his surroundings as a dog might. Mark is a hybrid between man and animal on a metaphorical rather than literal level, evoking an aura of hybridity through his appearance and behavior. He may not be hideous or defy classical aesthetics in a literal way, but there is an inherent multiplicity to his person that mixes frames of reference and recalls the fluid categories of the grotesque. Watching him sleep "curled up like a puppy,"[24] one cannot help wondering how far this animal pose goes and how deeply it permeates his essence.

Sure enough, as the novel progresses, Mark's animal qualities assume greater prominence and take a negative turn, at times overtaking his humanity. During initial descriptions, Mark's animal nature appears almost endearing. His distaste for societal form and general comfort with himself and his body read like a breath of fresh air in a novel populated by old-fashioned and stuffy countryside folk. Yet as his relationship with Vera assumes center stage, Mark transforms from puppy to downright beast, and his distaste for societal norms leads to serious moral transgression. Irrespective of any feelings

22. Ibid., 7:262.
23. Ibid., 7:262–63.
24. Ibid., 7:281.

he might harbor for her, Mark is described as too preoccupied with his own sensual desires to take Vera's emotions and needs into account. He draws Vera to their usual meeting place on the precipice where he pressures her to give herself to him carnally, rejecting the idea of marriage as unnaturally binding. Unwilling to submit to the power of social institutions, Mark cites the laws of nature as they apply to all living beings. As he argues, nature virtually mandates free and unrestrained sexual impulses and sexual intercourse.

Whereas picking apples and walking around barefoot were innocuous displays of a natural and spontaneous existence, within the universe of Goncharov's novel, the sexual violation of Vera emerges as the act of a "beast." According to the narrator, when Vera first walks away from him, Mark "[strides] fiercely, like a wild beast balked by his prey."[25] Watching Vera depart, he seems to experience a nearly irresistible impulse to spring forward and violate her, thus drawing attention to his predatory instincts. When Vera finally turns around, Mark rushes toward her and carries her away "like a wild animal" might whisk away its "prey." Instead of a dog, a "wolf" appears, as Vera jokingly calls Mark. When Vera abandons him, Mark affirms his own predatory nature and describes himself as a "wolf" with "a fox's cunning and the malice of a yapping dog."[26] In combination, these qualities strip away much of Mark's humanity.

Although Goncharov does not recreate a full-blown grotesque aesthetic in his depiction of Mark, the animal qualities the author ascribes to him suggest an inherent dualism in the character. Mark dehumanizes human society, seeing it as a series of gnats, but is in turn dehumanized by the author and reduced to a predatory animal. His actions and worldview are so embedded in animalism that the hybridity of his nature pierces through his harmonious physique. The grotesque in Mark may be a mere hint, but the man-animal dualism, his materialism, and his aversion to spirituality begin a tradition of grotesque degradation and hybridity in Russian realism.

III. THE EVOLUTION OF GROTESQUE REALISM IN *CATHEDRAL FOLK*

A noticeable evolution and strengthening of grotesque motifs occurs in Russian realism in Leskov's *Cathedral Folk*. Whereas Goncharov primarily hints at the grotesque in Mark Volokhov's person, Leskov captures the aesthetics

---

25. Ibid., 7:618.
26. Ibid., 7:730.

of the grotesque more directly. Just as in *The Precipice,* in *Cathedral Folk* the grotesque is encountered in representations of nihilists like Varnava Prepotensky and Izmail Termosesov. Varnava closely resembles Mark Volokhov in his materialism, but it is the other nihilist, Izmail Termosesov, who seduces women. Indeed, in Leskov's depiction of the lecherous Termosesov the reader encounters the first full-blown manifestation of grotesque realism as a poetics and not merely an ideology of materialistic degradation.

Unlike Leskov's more polarizing novel, *At Daggers Drawn,* where the demonization of nihilists is the primary focus, *Cathedral Folk* centers on the lives and spiritual dilemmas of clergy in a small town. For this reason, Leskov scholars traditionally view this novel as a move away from his more polemical, anti-nihilist works. Even so, Leskov, who "could barely restrain his dislike of nihilism,"[27] engages in his usual attacks on the new men. Indeed, as some scholars have suggested, *Cathedral Folk* served as an aesthetic laboratory for the later nihilist figures that appear in *At Daggers Drawn.*[28]

Leskov's contemporaries and his critics have decried his depiction of nihilists in *Cathedral Folk* as "ridiculously exaggerated."[29] The reason in part is that against the neutral background of *Cathedral Folk,* Leskov's attacks of the new men are all the more transparent and vociferous. At the same time, this exaggeration was also a result of the poetics of grotesque realism that Leskov employed in his portrayal of the new men.

Leskov depicts two nihilist characters in the novel: Varnava Prepotensky, the science teacher at the local school, and Izmail Termosesov, a nihilist turned spy for the secret police. Varnava resembles both Turgenev's Bazarov and Goncharov's Volokhov. Like these other characters, Varnava is a true believer in materialism who perceives science as omniscient and capable of objectively explaining life's phenomena. His preference for scientific and material observation over all other forms of knowledge becomes apparent when a stranger's dead body washes up in town. Having learned about the incident, Varnava asks the chief of police to grant him possession of the dead body. While Bazarov dissected frogs to arrive at the materialist basis of human existence, Varnava extends his blind materialism to fellow human beings and dissects another man. Instead of burying the body, he carries out a series of unusual experiments that show no respect for the dead. From Leskov's nauseating descriptions, it is revealed that Varnava boils the body until the flesh falls off and a bare skeleton remains.

---

27. Wigzell, "Leskov's Soboryane: A Tale of Good and Evil in the Russian Provinces," 902.
28. Eekman, "Leskov's *At Daggers Drawn* Reconsidered," 207.
29. Wigzell, 902.

Witnessing these acts, one might view Varnava's desecration of the body as bearing a distinctly grotesque quality. His treatment of the corpse suggests that he perceives the dead body as a mere physical object with no human characteristics. Varnava himself may not be grotesque in appearance, but his worldview, like that of Volokhov, is deeply influenced by the ideas behind the grotesque. Instead of recognizing in this body a deceased fellow human being, Varnava degrades it to the level of bare physicality. The skeletal corpse is stripped of all humanity and emerges as a half-human, half-object creature.

While Varnava's materialism evokes the grotesque as a philosophical position, Leskov's depiction of Termosesov brings out the aesthetics of grotesque realism in the novel. Termosesov stands out as a grotesque being, personally embodying the hybridity and deformation that define the style. When he first arrives, the inhabitants of the town, including the saintly Tuberozov, are shocked by his unattractive appearance. "That man is thick-lipped and horrible," says Tuberozov after first seeing Termosesov.[30] Later, Termosesov is described as fleshy, and his thickset upper body is shown in its fullest grotesquery while he takes a bath.

Termosesov's disharmony is accentuated by the complete absence of proportionality in his physical appearance. At one point, emphasizing Termosesov's hybridity, Leskov compares the character to a centaur:

> Termosesov somewhat resembled a centaur. His huge masculine height was associated with a healthy but thoroughly feminine build; he was narrow in the shoulders, and disproportionately broad in the hips; his thighs were regular horse-hams; his knees were fleshy and round; his arms were thin and sinewy; his neck was long, but had no Adam's apple, as in the case of most adult men, but a hollow like a horse; his head had a mane which stood out in all directions; his face was swarthy, with a long, apparently Armenian nose, and with an enormous upper lip, which rested ponderously on the lower one; Termosesov's eyes were light-brown in hue with sharp, black spots in the pupils; his gaze was steadfast and intelligent.[31]

Termosesov's huge masculine height attenuated by a feminine build suggests the transgression of boundaries typical of the grotesque. Although we learn that Termosesov's gaze was "steadfast and intelligent,"[32] he is so patently base and degraded that he emerges as a grotesque "subject turned into flesh"— a collection of unidentifiable body parts, characterized by ugliness and

---

30. Leskov, *Sobranie sochinenii v odinatsati tomakh*, 4:152.
31. Ibid., 4:158.
32. Ibid.

unshapeliness. In his appearance, which emerges as a mixture between man, woman, and horse, Leskov gives poetic shape to the more theoretical hybridities encountered in Chernyshevsky's "On the Anthropological Principle in Philosophy" and Goncharov's *The Precipice*.

Because of the realist component of the text, Termosesov's hybridity cannot be literal. Rather, his centaur-like appearance is implicit and metaphorical; instead of truly having a centaur frame, Termosesov has a frame that resembles that of a centaur. Even so, the exaggerated equine and feminine characteristics of Termosesov mark a transition in Russian grotesque realism as the style assumes more distinct poetic outlines.

What is unique about Termosesov, aside from his hybridity, is the primal ugliness characterizing him. While he may share the mane-like hair of Goncharov's Mark Volokhov, Termosesov's physical appearance is a great deal more bestial and repulsive than Volokhov's. His large upper lip and Armenian nose, his fat thighs and fleshy knees do not simply add a horse-like quality to the character, but they embody the essential ugliness of the grotesque. A monstrous other in a way that the handsome Volokhov cannot be, Termosesov introduces an aesthetic of ugliness into Russian realism through his physical grotesquery. In this sense, *Cathedral Folk* is unique among the works Leskov penned against nihilists. Even in *At Daggers Drawn*, where Gordanov is described as a nihilist "not to the new but to the newest cult" and superior to "Bazarov, Raskolnikov, and Markushka Volokhov,"[33] the reader never encounters this level of unattractiveness. This exaggeration of Termosesov's appearance helps determine both the depiction of nihilists in the Russian literary scene and the future literary path of grotesque realism. Nihilists had been demonized and turned into bestial others before, but Leskov made them repulsive as well. This ugliness eventually moves beyond them, to be inherited by characters from other, more mainstream social groups in later works like Dostoevsky's *Demons*, Saltykov-Shchedrin's *The Golovlev Family*, and Tolstoy's *Resurrection*.

IV. NIHILISTS ANNIHILATING THE SOUL

The aesthetic of ugliness ascribed to nihilists was not an end in itself, but a retort and a reflection on the threat that writers believed nihilists and their materialism posed to Russia during the unstable period of the Great Reforms. If one thinks of the grotesque as a style of degradation that captures life

---

33. Leskov, *Na nozhakh*, 81.

deprived of spiritual meaning, then the figure of the soulless nihilist portends a crisis in the Russian subject, an inner contradiction between Russia's idealism and proverbial soulfulness and a new generation that saw everything on strictly physical terms. Writing during the late 1870s, Vladimir Solovev addresses the "unresolvable internal contradiction" he believed existed within the contemporary subject between the particular facts and phenomena of life, or natural conditions, and the absolute significance and rights he associates with human interiority.[34] Solovev's project was to find reconciliation between these divergent drives in the subject through the idea of divine humanity, which would later appeal to Russian realists like Tolstoy and Dostoevsky. Within the context of the anti-nihilist novel, however, we do not encounter any such attempts at reconciliation, but rather a pointed rejection of materialism as inferior and immoral through the grotesque. As anti-nihilist writers confronted the important tension between materialism and idealism, the grotesque became a tool for their condemnation of the nihilists' reductionist worldview and dismissal of God and religion.

Leskov and Goncharov capture this broader struggle within the Russian subject through nihilists that actively participate in the spiritual demise of others through crude materialism and faithlessness. In *The Precipice* Mark Volokhov is juxtaposed to the idealistic gentry characters, Tatyana Markovna and Tushin, who represent a principled world of traditional ideals and family, the very best of gentry values. Similarly, in *Cathedral Folk* nihilists face off against religious figures, like Father Tuberozov, who exhibits indefatigable faith, and the energetic and brawny deacon Akhila, in whom faith turns into outright pathos. In both novels, nihilists threaten the higher ideals of Russian spirituality with their grotesque worldview. In particular, we can see them extend their materialism to others to objectify and dehumanize them, which resolves the dilemma of the subject in materialistic terms.

One obvious such example is the sexual degradation and objectification of women, an important subplot in most anti-nihilist novels. Instead of initiating any sort of emotional relationship with women, many materialistic nihilists reduce romantic relationships to a purely carnal level without long-term emotional commitment or emotional exchange. Nihilists dehumanize their romantic interests and view them not as integrated persons in whom soul and body coexist harmoniously but as mere sexual objects.

The most pernicious example of nihilists objectifying women appears in Leskov's *Cathedral Folk,* where the nihilist villain Termosesov seduces women and then uses them for his nefarious schemes. His most significant conquest

---

34. *Lectures on Divine Humanity,* 17–19.

is the tax collector's wife, Madame Bizyukina. Thrilled to meet a truly pro-
gressive man in Termosesov, Bizyukina endeavors to paint a picture of herself
as a "new person." After a brief conversation with Termosesov, however, she
quickly discovers that he is working for the secret police. In his own words,
Termosesov holds that "in Russia power lies in government service, not in
Vera Pavlovna's workshops."[35] As his quip about Chernyshevsky's *What Is to Be
Done?* suggests, instead of dwelling on higher beliefs or revolutionary ideals,
Termosesov believes in nothing at all. Without heeding political questions, he
is interested only in pursuing a sexual relationship and propositions Madame
Bizyukhina almost immediately. Ignoring her words and convictions, he only
pays attention to her body, seizing her hands and then shamelessly planting a
kiss on her with his terrible, thick lips.

The objectification of women also assumes very pronounced form in the
case of Vera in *The Precipice* who is similarly deprived of her spirituality and
reduced to the level of a hybrid creature in Mark's gaze. Thinking of these
characters from the prism of the grotesque, they fall on opposite ends of the
spectrum. Mark possesses an animal nature, whereas Vera, who is deprived
of agency, assumes object-like status. Vera accuses Mark of "leaving her like a
thing"[36] when he loses interest in a platonic relationship with her. This statement suggests that Mark's sexual desire denies Vera basic psychological depth.
More references to Vera as a dead thing ensue after her relationship with Mark
is consummated. Shortly thereafter, she "sleeps like the dead."[37] Vera attempts
to smile at her sister, Marfa, but the narrator compares her eyes to "Kak u
mertvoi, kotoroi ne uspeli zakryt' glaz" [the eyes of a corpse that no one has
remembered to close].[38] At these times all the passionate spirituality and live-
liness that formerly animated Vera seem stifled. She even loses her commu-
nicative abilities and asks Raisky to speak to Tatyana Markovna on her behalf
about what transpired with Mark. In fact, Vera is so dehumanized that she
even longs for the peace that comes with being dead, asking for rest without
awakening.

Vera's longing for death, and the presentation of death as a divestment of
all emotion, point to a key image in anti-nihilist grotesque realism: the dead
body. The tensions between idealism and materialism come to a head in the
figure of the corpse, who seems like the quintessential grotesque other, emptied of consciousness and completely reduced to its material basis. In Leskov's
Cathedral Folk, the image of the corpse in Varnava's possession serves as an

---

35. Leskov, *Sobranie sochinenii v odinnatsati tomakh*, 4:161.
36. Goncharov, 7:614.
37. Ibid., 7:632.
38. Ibid., 7:633.

essential test of faith—the sight of the unburied dead calls into question not only the existence of God but also that of the human spirit. Varnava has taken a fellow human being and degraded him to the level of a classroom object that can be put on display. But while Varnava conceives of the corpse in purely materialistic terms and insists on keeping it aboveground for the purposes of study, others in town view his actions as a sacrilegious defiance of faith.

The treatment of the corpse and the general attack on spirituality carried out by Varnava capture the broader attack on religious faith carried out by nihilists. Individuals like Mark Volokhov, Varnava Prepotensky, and Izmail Termosesov echo the ideas of Moleschott, Vogt, and Büchner, whose slogan "no force without matter" suggested that thoughts and every part of the human being are potentiated by neurons and sheer biology.[39] These ideas, first shared with the Russian reading by Dobroliubov in *The Contemporary* (1858),[40] are reflected by nihilist characters in both *Cathedral Folk* and *The Precipice* who seek to define the human subject through materialism alone.

As we can see from both novels, nihilists used science to illustrate this idea, along with the implied conclusion that there could be no higher power in the world. In *Cathedral Folk* Varnava used to be a seminary student who opted to become a science teacher because he did not like feigning religious belief. Given the religious context of the novel and the deep religious spirituality of characters like Father Savely Tuberozov and Deacon Akhila, this rejection of God and spiritual life is deeply jarring. Fittingly, Varnava uses the corpse to disabuse schoolchildren of conventional ideas regarding faith and God's relationship to the world. As we learn from Father Tuberozov's diary, in order to convert the children to his materialist doctrine, Varnava identifies various bones on the human skeleton and challenges the students to physically locate the soul within the same structure. Unable to physically locate the soul in the body, the children question whether it exists, which in turn destabilizes their faith in God. This example, in which the ephemeral soul is assigned a concrete physical space, is an unsettling instance of grotesque degradation, as scientific evidence lowers everything to level of physicality.

Volokhov in *The Precipice* is similarly engaged in conversations with youths in town, shaking their spirituality and faith in God while extolling science and materialism as the most rational approach to reality. Engaged in what he calls a baptism of "living water," Volokhov convinces the local boys that there is no God.[41] Later, one of these same boys tells his mother that it is senseless to attend mass in church. Another boy preaches similar messages to

39. Frede, "Materialism and the Radical Intelligentsia: The 1860s," 79.
40. Ibid.
41. Goncharov, 7:525.

his servants and donates the materialism textbooks Volokhov has given him to the local bookstore in order to educate the public.

The influence nihilists hold and the damage they do to both women and especially children reveals the degree to which they threaten spirituality in Russia during the era of the Great Reforms. In demonizing nihilists and transforming them into grotesque others, Goncharov and Leskov were responding to this very threat. The creed of the nihilists—equated by anti-nihilist writers to faithlessness and the objectification of others—was not a self-contained phenomenon. In later works of grotesque realism, a worldview similar to that held by nihilists expanded and was espoused by entire communities. Although this evolution of the grotesque does not occur in these two anti-nihilist novels, the spreading of the nihilist message among children hints at the potential infectiousness of both nihilism and the grotesque.

V. OVERCOMING THE GROTESQUE NIHILIST

When faced with the society-wide threat of nihilists, both Goncharov and Leskov took appropriate measures to curb the impact of these characters. In both *The Precipice* and *Cathedral Folk* they limit the grotesque aesthetic to the new men, and, more importantly, they show that their influence on local society is neither fatal nor permanent. Given the different subject matters and aesthetic structures of *The Precipice* and *Cathedral Folk,* we can note two distinct approaches by Goncharov and Leskov. Within the more properly novelistic context of *The Precipice,* Goncharov marginalizes the nihilist and his impact on local society. *Cathedral Folk,* which, by Leskov's own admission is as much a chronicle as a novel, is somewhat looser, and instead of neutralizing the nihilist, Leskov counters his actions through a competing storyline.

Beginning with Goncharov, we know that his very aesthetic stance was aimed at diffusing the effects of fleeting historical phenomena for the sake of a larger truth. In discussions of the author's aesthetic philosophy, Milton Ehre argues that although Goncharov believed it was important to achieve "truth" in art, he insisted that this truth not be "mathematical truth." Instead, the author endeavored for a type of "artistic truth," inseparable from the "tones" and "illuminations" of eccentric imagination that deviated from the "truth of reality."[42] As Ehre points out, although Goncharov was conspicuously silent about them, his artistic philosophy was at least partly aimed at men of the 1860s like Chernyshevky and Pisarev and their followers. Goncharov called

---

42. Ehre, *Oblomov and His Creator: Life and Art of Ivan Goncharov,* 72.

these individuals "neorealists" or "ultrarealists" and viewed their realism as narrow, tendentious, and lacking in poetry with its focus on sterile topical concerns.[43] He countered their neorealist focus with his own brand of realism that captured permanent social fixtures and types. For Goncharov, literature should not treat the present but focus on phenomena and people "settled, stable, and formed over a long period of time."[44]

This aesthetic philosophy manifests itself in *The Precipice* where it helps contain the nihilist threat. Set in the 1830s, a period significantly removed from the time of the novel's writing and publication, *The Precipice* had sufficient temporal distance to observe a "settled and stable" gentry way of life. This distance meant that the novel's protagonist was not a contemporary figure like Mark Volokhov but rather the gentry idealist Raisky. His centrality shapes the aesthetic makeup of the novel at large and the superior role assigned to idealism. Elena Krasnoshchekova even goes so far as to describe Raisky, who is writing his own novel (titled *Vera*), as an artistic co-creator of parts of *The Precipice*.[45] Whether one agrees with this suggestion or not, it ultimately underscores the importance of idealism in *The Precipice*. Through the eyes of the nobleman Raisky, for whom idealism is an "ethical imperative," the Russian countryside is depicted in an idyllic light[46] as somehow immune to incursions from outside instability. Most importantly, the novel's gentry idealism helps marginalize Mark Volokhov's materialist worldview. Mark, who receives a fraction of the narrative space Raisky does, is a pariah who cannot be received by the town's society and is comfortable only in the bowels of the precipice.

Goncharov conceives of the precipice as a narrative safeguard for the novel's gentry society. In the earlier *Oblomov*, he had already created a comparable space through the gully, which contained negative phenomena and prevented them from invading the boundaries of Oblomovka. He similarly borders passions and other subversive drives in *The Precipice*. Within the bounds of the precipice, passions explode, people let loose, and conventional societal restraints are not respected; everything repressed, anything that would otherwise threaten social identity, is unfettered. As the text reveals, in recent years a man was buried in the precipice after murdering his wife, her lover, and eventually himself in a scene of primal jealousy.

This physical demarcation of the precipice ensures the preservation of gentry order in the novel. When characters with an established social identity,

---

43. Ibid., 74–75.
44. Ibid., 74.
45. Krasnoshchekova, *Ivan Aleksandrovich Goncharov: Mir tvorchestva*, 393–95.
46. Ibid., 397.

like Vera, embrace the temptation of the precipice, the transgression is usually temporary, and traditional values are eventually reaffirmed. After giving herself to Mark, Vera permanently returns to the societal fold, never to descend to the precipice again. She confesses everything to her aunt and eventually marries the landowner Tushin who is a practical, enterprising type, much like Stoltz in *Oblomov*. As traditional values are reaffirmed, the grotesque other, Mark Volokhov, leaves town, permanently ejected from the social realm. His values and personality, which evoke the grotesque within the text, do not leave any permanent marks on the local reality but fizzle out over time. Tatyana Markovna, the dowager gentry leader of the town, eventually undoes the precipice in its entirety by removing the arbor and clearing out the space. This reorganization suggests that the danger presented by the precipice has passed, as gentry order is restored unscathed.

When presenting destructive nihilists in *Cathedral Folk,* Leskov takes a somewhat different approach. In his more traditional anti-nihilist novel, *At Daggers Drawn (Na nozhakh)*, he provides an unexpected and stilted happy ending within the gentry sphere despite the terrible crimes of nihilists. The nihilist gentry bastard Gordanov is arrested and has his arm amputated, while the general's wife Sintyanina marries the landowner Podozerov. Within the looser constraints of the chronicle, in *Cathedral Folk* Leskov opts for a less formulaic narrative resolution. Without undoing the actions of nihilists or their grotesque materialism, he counters these actions through a parallel plotline that lionizes religious faith.

The most dangerous nihilist in Old Town, Termosesov, has close ties to the Third Section and denounces the archpriest Tuberozov as a revolutionary. Thanks to this denunciation, the saintly archpriest is removed from his post and dies in exile from his community. Although on the surface Leskov allows the nihilist Termosesov free rein in the novel, he eventually removes the character from Old Town and counters his grotesque realism with a story about the spiritual awakening of the feisty deacon Akhila. Until Father Tuberozov's death, Akhila approaches the world primarily through his strong body—he likes to drink and relies on his physical strength to resolve conflicts. However, as Faith Wigzell argues, after Father Tuberozov's death Akhila renounces "physical strength for spiritual wisdom, another kind of strength."[47] Having experienced a spiritual fall in St. Petersburg, where atheist friends convince him that God does not exist, Akhila remembers his faith and is shaken by the loss of Tuberozov.

---

47. Wigzell, 908.

Akhila's mourning is seemingly boundless. At one point, he refuses all food and drink, which reads like an ascetic denial of bodily comfort and bodily life for the sake of higher feelings. So extreme is Akhila's bereavement that he experiences "heightened sensitivity" in the form of acute and overwhelming emotionalism.[48] Leading up to his death, he incrementally displays greater awareness of the soul and shows great spiritual wisdom as his body burns up in fever. While on his deathbed, Akhila begins to understand that nothing material is worthy of much attention. Instead of lamenting the death of his body, he cites the Book of Revelation, asserting that since everything is destined to vanish, it is inappropriate to cling to material things. Akhila's death does not yield a happy ending to *Cathedral Folk,* but it showcases, at least for a time, a victory of soul over body. Unlike nihilists who espouse a grotesque worldview that reduces everyone and everything to the level of the body, Akhila chooses the soul, thus providing a counter-nihilist path in Leskov's novel and in the anti-nihilist genre at large. At the end of *Cathedral Folk* one gets the feeling that despite the damage done by Termosesov, faith and spirituality will be renewed in the town as new religious leaders arrive.

The nihilist characters in these novels—Mark Volokhov, Varnava Prepotensky, and Izmail Termosesov—are ultimately exiled from the traditional worlds they infiltrate and unsettle. However valiant their efforts, their actions are regulated or negated as traditional values are reaffirmed. For the most part, these values derive from traditional social groups like the gentry and clergy, who were afforded greater privileges in the old caste-like estate system. Through this reaffirmation of the gentry and clergy groups we can see a still-lingering traditional and conservative mentality in post-Emancipation Russia. The image of the part-human, part-animal nihilists reflect the demonization and dehumanization of outsiders in a society driven by such traditional mentalities. If in real life the socially amorphous *raznochintsy* group accommodated social diversity and the amalgamation of different social categories, in the anti-nihilist novel, this diversity, along with the equalizing materialist philosophy, became the seed for grotesque monstrosity. As the rest of this book reveals, however, while the grotesque was first employed as a means of stigmatizing outsiders in Russian realism, over time the style stretched to encompass traditional social groups.

---

48. Leskov, 4:316.

Members of the gentry estate, seen as pillars of traditional society in anti-nihilist novels, became a key target of the style. In this sense, Dostoevsky's *Demons* marks a transitional moment in the Russian novel's diachronic evolution. In Dostoevsky's work, the lens of the grotesque expands beyond nihilists and into depictions of gentry characters like Nikolai Stavrogin. In addition, Dostoevsky also stretches the scope of the style. Whereas in more traditional anti-nihilist works, nihilist outsiders enter a town and leave without producing consequential changes, Dostoevsky allows nihilists greater and more pernicious power, giving them the ability to transform the novelistic world into a grotesque microcosm and a reflection of themselves.

CHAPTER 2

NIHILIST MONSTERS AND THE FAILED GENTRY PROTAGONIST IN DOSTOEVSKY'S *DEMONS*

While Dostoevsky was writing the broader "religious poem"[1] *The Life of a Great Sinner,* disturbing events in his contemporary Russia moved him in a more tendentious, anti-nihilist artistic direction. Newspapers like Katkov's *Moskovskie vedemosti* published grizzly details from the 1869 murder of Ivan Ivanovich Ivanov by members of the revolutionary group *Narodnaya Rasprava* (*The People's Summary Justice*). Under the pretext that fellow group member Ivanov intended to denounce the organization to the secret police, the men killed him at the behest of their group leader, Sergei Nechaev. The police discovered the body in a nearby pond, weighed down with stones, and, soon enough, the Third Section caught up with the perpetrators. After Dostoevsky read about these terrible events, his indignation was so profound that he decided to condemn the crime through a tendentious novel, with no concern for artistry. "Let it turn out only a pamphlet," he wrote to Strakhov in 1870, "but I will express myself."[2]

These initial sentiments produced the significant anti-nihilist sections in *Demons* that centered on the murder and its perpetrators. When read alongside the tradition of anti-nihilist writings, *Demons* fits right in as a novel that

---

1. Mochul'skii, *Dostoevsky: His Life and Work,* 402.
2. Quoted in Mochul'skii, 407.

demonizes the new generation. This anti-nihilist core has as one of its main protagonists the archvillain and Nechaev stand-in, Pyotr Verkhovensky. Dostoevsky depicted the character as a petty monster through devices of grotesque realism similar to those encountered in novels like *The Precipice* or *Cathedral Folk*. But while engaging in conventional attacks on nihilists, Dostoevsky also significantly broadened the scope of the anti-nihilist novel and the nascent style of grotesque realism.

In *The Precipice* and *Cathedral Folk,* nihilists are perceived as a threat to spirituality and as a corrupting influence, steering children away from faith. As a timely genre developed in response to contemporary developments, the anti-nihilist novel grappled with this chaos by placing the blame for it on the shoulders of nihilists and presenting traditional gentry society as Russia's salvation. Goncharov's *The Precipice* is a good example of this strategy. Even Leskov's looser creations, *Cathedral Folk* and *At Daggers Drawn,* conclude with a restoration of order that washes away the mischief of grotesque nihilists. The nihilist threat to spirituality was an obvious concern for Dostoevsky as well. Aware of the instability befalling Russia during and after the Great Reforms, Dostoevsky discussed the state of affairs with nervous presentiment. "The foundations of society are cracking under the pressure of the revolution brought by the reforms," he wrote in 1874 in his notebooks to *The Adolescent.*[3]

As Goncharov's final restoration of order shows, despite timely anti-nihilist elements, novels like *The Precipice* were also intimately related to what Dostoevsky disparaged as landowner literature. Using Tolstoy's works as an example, Dostoevsky described landowner literature as a type of writing out of touch with tumultuous, contemporary Russia. In Dostoevsky's view, centered on gentry realities, landowner literature captured settings such as the peaceful world of the upper-class family where everything was stable and predictable. This sense of enduring stability that Dostoevsky associated with landowner literature is apparent in *The Precipice* where all glimpses of contemporary chaos are contained to the outskirts and harmony wins out over the disharmonious grotesque introduced by nihilists like Mark Volokhov.

As scholars have argued, Dostoevsky took it upon himself to express Russia's "social chaos" in most of his mature novels, which challenged this narrative appearance of harmony.[4] In many cases, he traces how this chaos also affected the poetics of his novels from the period.[5] In *Demons,* fittingly

---

3. Dostoevsky, *Polnoe,* 16:7.

4. Jackson, *Dostoevsky's Quest for Form: A Study of His Philosophy of Art,* 111.

5. For a fascinating look at how the societal instability of the Great Reforms affected Dostoevsky's novels from this period, see Kate Holland's recent study, *The Novel in the Age of Disintegration: Dostoevsky and the Problem of Genre in the 1870s.*

described as one of Dostoevsky's "most literary" works,[6] the author used grotesque realism to present his own version of the anti-nihilist novel. Studies of the grotesque in Dostoevsky's mature works are sparse, but the few existing ones suggest that the style facilitated aesthetic experimentation. The argument goes that Dostoevsky used the grotesque to "advance realism"[7] by foregrounding unnaturalness and oddity in order to avoid the compartmentalization and "oversimplification of human experience."[8] If in *The Precipice* there is a compartmentalization of good and evil and a sustained narrative order that combats the chaos of nihilists, Dostoevsky used the grotesque to show life as considerably more complicated. In his account, the dangers of nihilism are hardly so self-contained; instead, the new men's influence and their grotesquery poison the atmosphere of the whole novel.

From this perspective, *Demons* can be seen as a perfected incarnation of the anti-nihilist novel. Dostoevsky adopts the genre's basic mission of exposing the dangers of nihilism, which he fulfills more thoroughly than other authors. Scholars like Serge Gregory ascribe the superiority of *Demons* over other anti-nihilist novels to Dostoevsky's more successful plot and character development. I would suggest that is also Dostoevsky's willingness to allow nihilists to pull society into total chaos that makes *Demons* the apotheosis of the anti-nihilist genre. Moving away from realism's and the anti-nihilist novel's objective of showing the status quo as infallible, Dostoevsky highlights the pernicious threat of nihilists precisely by allowing them to upturn local society.

In the process, Dostoevsky also breaks down conventional anti-nihilist paradigms that glorified the gentry as the hope for society's salvation. *Demons* begins with a quiet and familiar novelistic reality comparable to that of the worlds that appear in landowner literature. Dostoevsky spends the remainder of the narrative unraveling this order to the point where it is irrecoverable. This disruption is carried out through the grotesque, which extends from the nihilist scapegoat, Pyotr Verkhovensky, to the novel's gentry protagonist, Nikolai Stavrogin. Although Stavrogin has the pedigree of a proper gentry character, he emerges as a grotesque distortion of such figures by not living up to his promise and abetting the nihilist cause. This transition in the grotesque from the nihilist figure to the gentry protagonist sets the stage for future depictions of gentry characters, like Saltykov-Shchedrin's Golovlev landowners, as grotesque others. Once the gentry hero turns into a morally vacuous, automaton-like character, the materialism and the lack of spiritual-

---

6. Saraskina, *"Besy": Roman-Preduprezhdenie*, 117.

7. Fanger, 125.

8. George Gibian, "The Grotesque in Dostoevsky," 268.

ity characteristic of the grotesque encompass the town as a whole. Dostoevsky stretches the grotesque's aesthetic, turning the novel's provincial reality into a postreform grotesque microcosm reminiscent of Saltykov-Shchedrin's Glupov.

I. AN AVERAGE TOWN

In interpretations of Dostoevsky's *Demons,* scholars have noted marked shifts and inconsistencies within the narrative, suggesting that there is an escalation in instability as the novel chronologically transitions between the three parts. Most notably, Jacques Catteau compares the novel to a Piranesi staircase with alternative plateaus and crescendos in narrative tension.[9] Dostoevsky himself confirms this narrative unevenness in an unpublished afterword in which he describes the aesthetics of *Demons* in the following list format: "Traditions, the literature of the gentry, ideas, suddenly chaos, people without form [liudi bez obraza]—they have no convictions, no science, no point of emphasis; they believe in the vague mysteries of socialism."[10] From Dostoevsky's list one can infer a disparity between the beginning of the novel, which features a reality driven by order—"traditions, literature of the gentry"—and the anarchy created later with the incursion of "people without form." These contrasting forces recall the narrative conflicts encountered in other anti-nihilist novels as the order of traditional society clashes with the chaos unleashed by nihilists. Although Dostoevsky represents both, as his description suggests, it is only against this baseline of order that the dangers of nihilism can be fully foregrounded.

Dostoevsky carefully constructs this initial stability in the early portions of part 1 of *Demons.* The novel begins in the heart of provincial Russia, possibly in Tver', a space described as a "quintessentially average" town.[11] "Very strange events," writes the chronicler at the beginning of the book, "took place in our town, hitherto not remarkable for anything [dosele nichem ne otlichavshem-sya gorode]."[12] Since the space is bound to the people occupying it and created through their perceptions and moods,[13] the town inhabitants appear no less average at first. The lives of Stepan Trofimovich, Varvara Petrovna, and

9. Catteau, *Dostoyevsky and the Process of Literary Creation,* 357.

10. Dostoevsky, 11:308.

11. Lounsbery, "Dostoevskii's Geography: Centers, Peripheries, and Networks in *Demons,*" 212.

12. Dostoevsky, *Polnoe sobranie* 10:8. I use the Richard Pevear and Larissa Volokhonsky translation of *Demons,* 8. All subsequent citations will list the English translation first and then the volume and page number from the Russian edition of Dostoevsky's full works.

13. Catteau, 420.

the town's liberal circle convey a sense of stability and tradition. No one could expect a grizzly crime like Ivanov's murder to occur in such a peaceful place inhabited by agreeable people. Fittingly, the tranquil town is run by a permissive governor, Ivan Osipovich, a kind and philandering old man who defers to the moral authority of his cousin, Varvara Petrovna, on most matters. Unlike later, when political manifestos are distributed among factory workers, in the early part of the novel there are no anxieties about stability or any apparent need for policing crime.

Compounding the aura of ennui and the expectation of stability, Dostoevsky's chronicler repeatedly insists that most inhabitants are ineffectual, jolly liberals. Anton Lavrentevich knows many inhabitants and, through his inside knowledge, often "reduce[s] the turbulent events of the book to eccentric and isolated manifestations."[14] The chronicler is particularly informed about Stepan Trofimovich, a washed-up liberal of the 1840s, based on the historian T. N. Granovsky. Until their close ties peter out, Stepan is exclusively portrayed through his friend's subjective perspective as a harmless old man incapable of real action. Indeed, Anton Lavrentevich refutes the possibility of any political rebellion in town through his assurances that Stepan will never act and that his liberal circle is innocuous and politically insignificant. He views the town liberals, with Stepan Trofimovich at the helm, as an embodiment of the dictum that a "higher liberal" in Russia means "liberal bez vsyakoi tseli" [a liberal without aim].[15]

The only perceptible narrative goals in this early part of the novel are romantic in nature. Like in many works by Turgenev that chronicle gentry lives, love and romantic attachment arise as central forces in *Demons*. The chronicler focuses on Stepan Trofimovich's two marriages, his long flirtation with Varvara Petrovna, and his potential arranged marriage to Dasha. Other members of the liberal circle are also almost exclusively described in terms of their romantic affairs. There is mention of Shatov's unsuccessful marriage, Virginsky's romantic turmoil when his wife takes Lebyadkin as a lover, and Liputin's domineering nature as a husband. When not engaged in idle chats, card games, and drinking, the town liberals either disseminate romantic gossip or tend to their own turbulent romantic lives.

In the beginning of *Demons*, instead of focusing on the social and political changes produced by the Great Reforms, including the emergence of nihilists and terrorists like Nechaev, Dostoevsky concentrates the narrative on the restricted reality he found wanting in landowner literature—an isolated

---

14. Frank, "The Masks of Stavrogin," 661.
15. Dostoevsky, *Demons*, 33; 10:30.

corner of Russian life populated by members of the gentry and the upper middle class. But even as he recreates features of landowner literature, Dostoevsky simultaneously hints at the shortcomings of this restricted emphasis on a small slice of life. A clear alienation can be felt as the chronicler fixates on the posturing and hysterics of Stepan and Varvara while significant historical events go unnoticed on the sidelines. For instance, the chronicler hardly remarks on the 1861 Emancipation Manifesto. Instead of acquiring a broad view of the emancipation's impact on Russian society, we experience the event from the narrow-minded perspective of provincial inhabitants. St. Petersburg is abuzz with political news, but Stepan and Varvara feel alienated there. The reader experiences a meta-alienation when confronted with the duo's trivial concerns while tumultuous historical changes are taking place.

II. *"C'EST UN MONSTRE"*

The only element missing from the picture of stability conjured in the first few chapters of *Demons* is a proper nobleman protagonist.[16] As Dostoevsky ironically declares at the end of *The Adolescent* a few years later, if Russian novelists had any hope of conjuring "vid krasivogo poryadka i krasivogo vpechatleniya" [the appearance of a beautiful order and a beautiful impression], they had to take their protagonists from gentry stock.[17] Accordingly, an apparently beautiful gentry hero seems to materialize in *Demons* in the figure of Stepan Trofimovich's student and Varvara Petrovna's son, Nikolai Stavrogin. Young, handsome, well-mannered, of marriageable age, and a member of the gentry, Stavrogin enters the novelistic scene as the ultimate landowner hero. This image of Stavrogin is perpetuated during his return to the province when he is described as the "most elegant gentleman" who can make polite conversation and generally "observe [. . .] provincial etiquette with unflagging attention."[18] Stavrogin occupies the attention of everyone in town as both men and women are equally drawn to him.

Yet whereas Stavrogin fills a vacuum in *Demons* by occupying the role of landowner protagonist, his arrival is also what first upsets provincial ennui and the novel's fragile stability. Even before nihilist disorder takes root in the

---

16. The narrator expresses in no uncertain terms that Stepan Trofimovich is not a member of the nobility, and even Varvara Petrovna's gentry status dims when the text divulges that her family wealth has been accrued primarily through alcohol sales.

17. I am using the Pevear and Volokhonsky English translation of *The Adolescent*, 561. *Polnoe sobranie sochinenii*, 13:453.

18. Ibid., 44; 10:37.

novel, the breakdown of traditional literary paradigms is evident, as Stavrogin does not help uphold gentry order. Instead he displays a hybrid, multilayered selfhood that disrupts the novel's texture and paves the way for nihilist disorder. If Dostoevsky believed that disorder would proceed from grotesque "people without form," then the purported gentry hero, Stavrogin, exhibits this very formlessness.

Dostoevsky sets the stage for Stavrogin's grotesquery as early as the novel's epigraph, which encapsulates hybridity and formlessness through the story of the man possessed by a demon. The quote from the Gospel of Luke about the episode with the Gadarene swine introduces the idea of hybridity through descriptions of demonic possession.[19] The possessed men are quintessential grotesque hybrids, estranged from themselves, unable to dress properly, driven into cave isolation by demons; they are themselves but also objectified, grotesque beings lacking in agency who act out the will of others.

This image of the possessed man embodies the concept of fragmented identity in the novel, which is essential to how Stavrogin's plotline unfolds. Like the demonic man, Stavrogin's sense of self is fragmented, severed between a proper social self and an alien and irrational self. Alongside the gentry gentleman he sometimes shows himself to be, there is another, irrational and uncontrollable side to Stavrogin that comes out to undermine his attempts at civility. His time in St. Petersburg, where he was "living in strange company" in "dark slums and God knows what corners"[20] brings out this darker self. Details of his wild days cloud Stavrogin's image, suggesting that he may have more of a footing in the slums of Dostoevsky's St. Petersburg novels like *Crime and Punishment* than in the seemingly uneventful provincial reality of *Demons.*

Stavrogin's dualism and his unusual and unmotivated actions suggest the potential for grotesque hybridity in him. This hybridity is also reflected in his appearance, which triggers the grotesque by alluding to great irregularity. The chronicler, who elaborates on the character's unusual and seemingly inhuman face, describes Stavrogin's mien as follows:

> I was also struck by his face: his hair was somehow too black, his bright eyes were somehow too calm and clear, his complexion was somehow too delicate and white, the color of his cheeks was somehow too bright and clear, his teeth were like pearls, his lips like coral—you might say he was the picture of beauty, but at the same time there was also something repellent about him. They said his face resembled a mask [*masku*].[21]

19. Ibid., 8; 10:32–35.
20. Ibid., 42; 10:36.
21. Ibid., 43; 10:37.

The familiar components of Stavrogin's face—his eyes, teeth, and lips—are unnatural alongside one another, granting his face the look of a mask. This type of exaggerated attractiveness recalls the doll-like automaton, the quintessential human object, even though he has all the makings of a gentry hero. Much like the dazzling automaton Olympia in Hoffmann's "The Sandman," Stavrogin's beauty borders on the repulsive because it assumes inhuman, mask-like qualities. In Hoffmann's story, the automaton betrayed its inhumanity through her dead soulless eyes, eventually removed by her maker. By contrast, Stavrogin's inhumanity radiates from his entire face, which is sedate and ornamented to the point of resembling an inorganic mask. Over time, his mask-like appearance grows even more exaggerated and distinctly artificial. Falling asleep while sitting down on the couch early in part 2, Stavrogin appears "quite frozen, motionless" and "decidedly resembles an inanimate wax figure."[22]

The grotesquery extends beyond Stavrogin's appearance when he engages in uncouth behaviors that upend the "beautiful order" and the "beautiful impression" that define noblemen protagonists. According to the chronicler, during his visit in town, Stavrogin participates in three acts "beyond the bounds of all accepted conventions and measures":[23] he pulls the elder Gaganov by the nose, kisses Liputin's wife, and bites the ear of the local governor. All these actions appear unconscious, automated, and out of keeping with the novel's opening atmosphere. Describing Stavrogin's state of mind when he performs these acts, the chronicler mentions that "He [Stavrogin] was almost in a reverie, as if he had lost his mind."[24] These behaviors do not correspond with his gentry identity but seem more appropriate for the part of his self that is slum-bound. The strange, unmotivated biting is simultaneously automatized and animalistic and underscores a hybridity within Stavrogin similar to those found in proper anti-nihilist novels. "*C'est un monstre*" ["he is a monster"] exhorts Stepan Trofimovich when news spreads of Stavrogin having sold his estate to Captain Lebyadkin.[25] At other times, the chronicler also refers to Stavrogin as either a "beast"[26] or a "monster,"[27] thus evoking the beastliness and monstrosity encountered in anti-nihilist fiction.

When Stavrogin reveals his hybrid, grotesque self, all the instability repressed in the first part of *Demons* becomes unleashed. He completes the picture of gentry mirage in *Demons* and destroys it all at the same time.

---

22. Ibid., 223; 10:182.
23. Ibid., 50; 10:43.
24. Ibid., 45; 10:38.
25. Ibid., 121; 10:98.
26. Ibid., 45; 10:38.
27. Ibid., 51; 10:43.

Whereas in earlier works of anti-nihilism, the monster was almost always the nihilist other, in *Demons* that appellation is redirected toward the gentry protagonist. No longer an outsider in the margins of society, the monster has grown into the double of the town's gentry scion. Stavrogin wavers between worlds, a grotesque hybrid, alternating the roles of gentry landowner and monstrous slum king. Like the monstrosity of the possessed man, his hybridity is hidden from the naked eye—it is a prosaic monstrosity typical of grotesque realism.

III. A "NEW STORY"

Dostoevsky himself articulates Stavrogin's hybridity and dualism when thinking back to *Demons* in an 1875 notebook entry from *The Adolescent*. As he writes, Stavrogin is capable of "*two ways of acting* at one and the same time; in one form of action (with certain people) he is a more righteous man, with all his heart [. . .] In the other form of action he is a terrifying criminal, liar and debauchee (with different people)."[28] In this comment, Dostoevsky describes the duality characterizing Stavrogin and, through him, the novel as a whole. The narrative of *Demons* fluctuates depending on which elements of himself Stavrogin chooses to put on display. When the chronicler declares that a "*new story [novaya istoriya]*"[29] is about to begin early in part 2, he signals that this story is intimately tied to Stavrogin's actions.

Indeed, the new story begins when, in what resembles a symbolic escape from civilization, Stavrogin leaves the gentry quarters of his mother's estate through a back door in the middle of the night. He reaches the Filippov house on the other side of town and eventually goes as far as Zarechie. The transition from one space to the other manifests itself as a journey from order into chaos: "The road went downhill," explains the chronicler, "his feet slid in the mud, a wide, misty as if empty space opened out suddenly—the river. Houses turned into hovels, the street vanished into a multitude of disorderly lanes [ulitsa propala vo mnozhestve besporyadochnykh zakolukov]."[30] With its messy lanes and hovels, where divisions evaporate, Zarechie evokes not only mere disorder but also the social chaos of postreform Russia where the gentry estate is no longer separate from the rest of the population. Stavrogin's transition into Zarechie suggests his own and the novel's contemporaneous move away from traditional societal order.

---

28. Dostoevsky, *The Notebooks for* A Raw Youth, 27.
29. Emphasis mine. Dostoevsky, *Demons,* 217; 10:173.
30. Ibid., 257; 10:203.

There are several other moments when Stavrogin's hybridity, as character-ized by his behavioral inconsistency, affects the direction taken by the novel. Many characters perceive Stavrogin's role as that of a true nobleman, someone who, to borrow Dostoevsky's own expression, embodies the "beautiful order and beautiful impression" of the gentry. There are extensive discussions of nobility in the novel—Stepan Trofimovich addresses the "remarkable moral nobility of some knights,"[31] while Maria Timofeevna has in her possession a book about medieval knights. The question of whether Stavrogin himself pos-sesses such values becomes significant when both Maria and other characters look to him as a person of higher morality.

Both Stavrogin's gentry status and his nobility of spirit are tested when he meets the former serf and murderer, Fedka. During this encounter, Stav-rogin has the opportunity to restrain Fedka, who admits to killing the beagle of a church he robbed. At one point, Stavrogin seems to rise to the occasion by binding Fedka's hands with his scarf and tying him to a bridge. Yet he strangely regrets this action and eventually frees Fedka, even encouraging him to "Rezh' eshchyo, obokradi eshchyo" [kill more, steal more].[32] This surprise turn in Stavrogin highlights his grotesque hybridity. During this moment, it is as though his darker grotesque self rises to the surface, preferring chaos and social upheaval to order and restraint. There is the nobleman Stavrogin, who has the ability to set a moral standard in town, and the despiritualized, waxy automaton Stavrogin who facilitates crimes.

Almost always, it appears that despite the best of intentions, the unfeeling side of Stavrogin wins out. Drawn to chaos, Stavrogin emerges as an inad-equate gentry protagonist, a pretender in a novel that for a time also pretends to depict the more orderly realities of gentry society. His status as grotesque hybrid and sham protagonist is most clearly revealed in his marriage to the mentally disturbed Maria Timofeevna. Instead of having a proper romantic plot, Stavrogin has a farce of a marriage with extraordinary implications given that he is a member of the endogamous gentry estate. As late as the turn of the nineteenth century there was "oceanic"[33] distance among the gentry and virtually every other social group in Russian society, including the clergy. The reader never learns much about the social identity of the Lebyadkins, but since they meet Stavrogin in the slums of St. Petersburg, they likely belong to the *meshchane,* or the urban poor, and are complete outsiders to the tradi-tional estate system. In fact, the marriage is in such complete defiance of all

---

31. Ibid., 9; 10:9.
32. Ibid., 280; 10:221.
33. Etkind, *Internal Colonization: Russia's Imperial Experience,* 116.

social expectations that Stavrogin views escape to Switzerland as the only way to sustain the union.

Stavrogin's defiance of and failure in his role as gentry protagonist, as epitomized in his unbinding of Fedka and his marriage to Maria Timofeevna, precipitate the breakdown of gentry order in the novel and facilitate the fulfillment of Pyotr Stepanovich's conception of revolution. During the gathering of the revolutionary society later in the novel, Pyotr Stepanovich advocates precisely the "un[tying] of all hands" [razvyazhet ruki][34] that Stavrogin performs with Fedka. This narrative echo points to the ways in which Stavrogin ultimately facilitates Pyotr's designs and, metatextually, the way he potentiates the anti-nihilist plot.

Pyotr and Stavrogin arrive in the novelistic world together and vie for dominance from the very beginning. The two characters stand for the two divergent literary paths that ultimately combine in order to generate the sum total of Dostoevsky's novel, with both its anti-nihilist, pamphlet element and the parts fueled by Dostoevsky's plans for *Life of a Great Sinner*. These two characters—the gentry protagonist, Stavrogin, and the man from a mixed social background, Pyotr—would be perfect antagonists facing off and trying to thwart one another in conventional anti-nihilist novels. For instance, Raisky and Tushin are the gentry counterparts to Mark Volokhov in *The Precipice*. Dostoevsky recreates this antagonism in *Demons*, but instead of countering Pyotr, Stavrogin facilitates his plans.

Although Stavrogin does not directly enable Pyotr's crimes, he allows them to occur through his passivity and absence. As scholars have noted, after his nighttime journey to Zarechie and duel with Gaganov, Stavrogin fades out and is "relegated to the second plane."[35] His most significant appearance in the second half of the novel occurs in part 3 during the consummation of his relationship with Liza, which reads like a classic anti-nihilist plot turn, similar to the consummation of the relationship between Vera and Mark Volokhov in *The Precipice*. Like Mark, Stavrogin degrades Liza, turning her into a hysterical wreck in a dirty dress. Although Vera is redeemed and resurrected from her sexual objectification through a gentry husband in *The Precipice,* there is no such redemption for Liza, who soon walks to her death in the fire mob scene. The sexual escapade fits so well with the anti-nihilist genre that one might say that at the novel's conclusion, Stavrogin's former role as a gentry protagonist is completely eliminated, and he is given a place in Pyotr's anti-nihilist plot. "I've been inventing you since abroad," says Pyotr to Stavrogin referring to

---

34. Dostoevsky, *Demons,* 408; 10:315.
35. Mochul'skii, 409.

their time in Europe together.[36] By the novel's end, Stavrogin is nothing more than this invention.

IV. THE ANTI-NIHILIST GROTESQUE

Stavrogin's reduction to a passive bystander in Pyotr's plot, his grotesque distortion as gentry protagonist, and his transformation into an animalistic, soulless automaton, or a "living corpse," as Joseph Frank calls him,[37] estranges and derails the familiar "landowner" narrative at the beginning of *Demons*. In order for a landowner narrative to function, it requires a protagonist, and Stavrogin fails to live up to the high expectations of this role. He fails socially in part 1, and he fails morally in the rest of the novel. He is aware of everything that will happen—the murders of Maria, her brother, and Shatov—but ultimately cannot bring himself to stop those crimes.

So instead of Stavrogin, it is Pyotr who emerges as a main protagonist in the novel. Pyotr enters the world of *Demons* on Stavrogin's coattails, gaining the confidence of Varvara Petrovna and others through his ability to provide an alibi for Stavrogin and his behaviors. Having permeated the social sphere, he functions like Stavrogin's shadow—anticipating his needs and clearing his name at every turn. This supportive role eventually turns into a usurping one, as Pyotr becomes the true pretender of the novel, seeking to assume Stavrogin's place and his plotline. Like an underground, demonic self, Pyotr becomes the *enfant terrible* of the local gentry circle while Stavrogin performs a vanishing act. Everyone suspects that Pyotr may have connections to the revolutionary movement, but many are drawn to him precisely for these connections. One of Pyotr's main supporters is the wife of the new governor, Yulia Mikhailovna, who believes she is mentoring Pyotr and tempering his revolutionary tendencies.

Although Pyotr might assume the pose of landowner protagonist in society, Dostoevsky renders him as fundamentally grotesque, an empty shell of a person, driven solely by hunger for power. Pyotr's doctrine of power and manipulation was inherited from his historical counterpart, Sergei Nechaev. While Dostoevsky did not seek to make Pyotr an accurate historical double for Nechaev,[38] the writer attributed many of the latter's appalling ideas from "Catechism of a Revolutionary" to Pyotr. Likely cowritten with Mikhail Bakunin,

---

36. Dostoevsky, *Demons*, 423; 10:326.

37. Frank, "The Masks of Stavrogin," 670.

38. In fact, scholars have noted that Dostoevsky's creation is quite different from the real Nechaev, who was known for being remarkably antisocial, "pathologically touchy," and unable

this document gives the revolutionary a road map for social manipulation, disingenuousness, total depersonalization, and subservience to the cause. In the manifesto, the revolutionary is described as someone who

> must live within society while pretending to be completely different from what he really is, for he must penetrate everywhere, into all the higher and middle-classes, into the houses of commerce, the churches, and the palaces of the aristocracy, and into the worlds of the bureaucracy and literature and the military, and also into the Third Division and the Winter Palace of the Czar.[39]

The description of the revolutionary as a person with no allegiances pretending to be someone else at all times equates him to an empty vessel for the cause. The revolutionary is stripped of all alliances and, indirectly, all sense of self. As the example of Pyotr so clearly reveals, the "Catechism" model also divested the revolutionary of any concrete sociopolitical ideology other than longing for chaos and disorder. Through the caricature of the power-hungry Pyotr, who seeks nothing more than self-aggrandizement, Dostoevsky also shows the revolutionary as altogether deprived of spirituality. With his utter lack of moral principles and human connections except for his shallow and utilitarian adulation of Stavrogin, Pyotr is dehumanized and reduced to a grotesque shell for revolutionary power.

Further elements of the grotesque as it originates in the anti-nihilist genre adorn Dostoevsky's portrayal of Pyotr. Echoing works like *The Precipice* and *Cathedral Folk,* Dostoevsky shows Pyotr to be physically repulsive. In the title of the chapter introducing him, the character is called a serpent, a standard description for nihilists. In the course of introducing the character, Dostoevsky assigns serpent- and animal-like qualities to Pyotr. When Pyotr speaks, the chronicler describes this process in strictly anatomical terms,[40] dwelling on the description of his tongue, which commands attention by seemingly jutting outward. "You somehow begin to imagine," writes the chronicler, "that the tongue in his mouth must be of some special form, somehow unusually long and thin, terrible red, and with an extremely sharp, constantly and involuntarily wriggling tip."[41] Pyotr's sharp, red, and wriggling tongue, which protrudes into the world, is fundamentally grotesque because it disrupts the

---

to "tolerate people who [were] his equals" or stronger (quoted in Kelly, *Mikhail Bakunin: A Study in the Psychology and Politics of Utopianism,* 261).

39. Nechaev, "Revolutionary Catechism," 82.
40. Dostoevsky, *Demons,* 180; 10:144.
41. Ibid.

harmony of his personhood. In Bakhtin's definition, the grotesque body is distinguished precisely through its apertures and outward protrusions: "the open mouth, the genital organs, the breasts, the phallus, the potbelly, the nose."[42] These orifices and appendages on the body are emphasized because they disturb the classical vision of the person as a finished entity. In the case of Pyotr, in direct juxtaposition with Stavrogin who is closed and ossified to the point of resembling an object, the red, snake-like tongue is a breach in his armor of articulate chatter and false self-presentation. These elements of the tongue allude to the animal, making Pyotr into a grotesque hybrid of half-man and half-snake. Though he may attempt to politely infiltrate Varvara's drawing room, the description of his grotesque tongue implies that Pyotr is just as much of an aberration within that space as Stavrogin with his mask-like face.

In the context of grotesque realism, Pyotr's animalism cannot be overt or literal; rather, it is implicit and metaphorical. The red tongue only hints at animalism. Besides the few descriptions above, Pyotr's grotesquery is more visible on a psychological and metaphorical level, as Dostoevsky recreates much of Pyotr's grotesque monstrosity and animalism in his behaviors. As Bakhtin argues, "Eating and drinking are one of the most significant manifestations of the grotesque body."[43] Like Turgenev's Bazarov or Goncharov's Mark Volokhov who brazenly demand food, Pyotr has a utilitarian mindset and is very focused on eating. No doubt also playing on Chernyshevsky's new man Rakhmetov from *What Is to Be Done?* Dostoevsky shows Pyotr consuming food with gusto throughout the novel. Rakhmetov was extremely ascetic; he exercised, slept on nails, and ate only bread and rare, nearly raw steaks for his nourishment. Many Russian revolutionaries emulated him, including Nechaev, who slept on bare boards and ate only bread.[44] In his descriptions of Pyotr, Dostoevsky emphasizes the more nauseating elements of Rakhmetov's diet.

Pyotr's eating habits paint a larger picture of him as a grotesque, animalistic figure. At various points throughout the novel, his consumption of food punctuates his crimes, giving him a predatory bent. For instance, in the third part of the novel, after having planned Shatov's murder, Pyotr enters a tavern to eat a nearly raw beefsteak, which he savors much to Liputin's disgust. When coaxing Kirillov into taking upon himself the crimes of the fivesome—right after Shatov's murder and before Kirillov's suicide—Pyotr again eats with great pleasure. He asks whether he can help himself to Kirillov's leftover chicken,

---

42. Bakhtin, *Rabelais,* 26.
43. Ibid., 281.
44. Drozd, *Chernyshevskii's* What Is to Be Done?: *A Reevaluation,* 114.

since Kirillov will die soon, and Pyotr "had hardly any dinner at all."[45] At this time, he falls with "extraordinary greediness" upon the food.[46]

This ravenous food consumption at times when human lives are lost or destroyed suggests a disturbing, animal-like lack of conscience. How can one ask for chicken after having murdered another man? Pyotr has the ability to destroy the world around him and still take pleasure in a bountiful meal without the slightest pangs of conscience. His food consumption may be seen as a grotesque degradation of spiritual reality to the level of food. His utter lack of remorse and shock bring to mind the behaviors of predatory animals that can kill their prey with impunity and consume it afterwards. Unable to confront the true emotional or moral content of events, Pyotr acts like a wild animal, concerned only with physical subsistence. His behavior facilitates a mix of the animal and human frames of reference in him, which evokes the grotesque.

Pyotr's hybridity fits well with the animalistic image of the nihilist forged in the anti-nihilist novel, which formed the original and more polemical design of *Demons*. Pyotr appears as a proper nihilist villain, a hybrid, monstrous being with sinister goals. Yet, as the discussion of Stavrogin as a grotesque being already indicates, unlike in conventional anti-nihilist novels like *The Precipice* or *Cathedral Folk*, in *Demons* grotesque monstrosity is not limited to the nihilist. As a result, not only is there no gentry protagonist to counter Pyotr, but, as evidenced by the incident of the second lieutenant biting his superior on the shoulder, Kirillov biting Pyotr's finger before the suicide, or Shigalyov's animalistic apperance with his long ears, the scope of the grotesque is even broader, extending beyond the nihilist villain and the gentry protagonist. Instead of settling for the isolated grotesque person or persons like in *The Precipice* or *Cathedral Folk*, Dostoevsky expands grotesque realism in *Demons*, creating a grotesque microcosm. The harmonious gentry order with which the novel begins completely unravels as the narrative succumbs to complete chaos. It is by capturing this complete disorder of postreform Russia that Dostoevsky fully reveals the danger that nihilists present to his contemporary society, as the irrevocable destruction of gentry order drives this message home.

V. THE GROTESQUE MICROCOSM

The societal disorder and disintegration Dostoevsky believed resulted from the "pressure of the revolution brought by the reforms,"[47] can be readily wit-

---

45. Dostoevsky, *Demons*, 611; 10:464.
46. Ibid.
47. Dostoevsky, *Polnoe*, 16:7.

nessed in the later portions of *Demons* as chaos envelops the town and spirituality gives way to a materialistic, grotesque worldview. While Goncharov
and Leskov use the grotesque to show nihilists plagued by materialism, Dostoevsky stretches the grotesque style beyond a few distinct characters to reveal
virtually everyone as infected by this mentality. Throughout part 3 of the
novel, chaos seemingly overwhelms postreform Russian society, as everyone
espouses the grotesque soullessness brought to the town by Pyotr.

The sense of social disintegration in *Demons* implied in the Pushkin poem
from the novel's epigraph becomes apparent, as the town succumbs to Pyotr
Verkhovensky's influence. But while it may indeed be the case that, as the epigraph suggests, a demon is leading the townspeople, the people themselves
seem more than willing to follow the demon. Many of the "new people" in
the novel, such as Shigalyov with his large ears or Kirillov with his distorted
speech are in some way deeply disharmonious. Echoes of the grotesque originate with Pyotr's animalism and resonate with these other characters in the
novel. Indeed, over time, the novelistic world is contaminated by their grotesquery. By part 3 of *Demons* there is a complete narrative about-face—any
semblance of landowner literature gives way to a disorder informed by the
aesthetic philosophy of grotesque realism.

In this sense Dostoevsky breathes new life to grotesque realism and
expands it beyond the confines of more conventional anti-nihilist novels.
While anti-nihilist writers managed to depict nihilists as monsters with grotesque attributes, they never succesfully extended grotesque estrangment past
the limited scope of a few characters. For instance, in comparing *Demons* to
Krestovsky's *Panurge's Flock* (1869), which is quite similar thematically, Serge
Gregory notes an interesting difference between the two works that underscores the grotesque elements of Dostoevsky's work. "Dostoevsky's intentions
do not differ greatly from Krestovskii's when it comes to characterizing the
actions of nihilists," writes Gregory, "but Dostoevsky is able to dramatize
the chaos, whereas Krestovskii can only point his finger at it."[48] Dostoevsky
"dramatize[s] the chaos" and the nihilists' destruction of traditional structures
by extending the anti-nihilist grotesque to the rest of the novelistic world.
Instead of encountering a grotesque person or persons, by part 3 of the novel,
the entire town in *Demons* has turned into a grotesque microcosm where
everyone's behavior is motivated by the desire for grotesque degradation.

The transformation of the town from a quiet backwater into a grotesque
microcosm happens gradually after Pyotr's arrival, as the uneasy order found
in the novel's beginnings succumbs to disintegration. As the chronicler notes,
a mischievous and at times cruel playfulness overtakes many in town as they

48. Gregory, 450.

renounce both propriety and spirituality for the sake of a good laugh. "Strange was the state of people's minds at that time," he writes. "A certain frivolity emerged . . . something light and happy-go-lucky. . . . A certain disorderliness of mind became fashionable."[49] In describing this altered state of mind, the chronicler invokes Saltykov-Shchedrin's famous *The History of a Town* and suggests that the town has become Glupov-like, plagued by scandals and mischief.[50]

The description of the provincial town as a Glupov implies a similarity between Dostoevsky's *Demons* and Saltykov-Shchedrin's *The History of a Town*. Irrespective of whether Dostoevsky recognized *The History of a Town* as an example of grotesque realism, he recreates the narrative mood from Saltykov-Shchedrin's chronicle in *Demons*. If landowner literature provided a model for part 1 of *Demons,* and the anti-nihilist genre helped Dostoevsky launch his attack against nihilists, the remaining components of the novel borrow from Saltykov-Shchedrin's work of grotesque realism, which provided an example of a grotesque microcosm.

In Saltykov-Shchedrin's narrative of Glupov's history, the collective mentality is characterized by thoughtlessness, impulsivity, and outright longing for anarchy. At one point, the citizens of Glupov fail to tend to their crops and starve as a result; another time they adopt paganism; they flock to or rebel against their leaders for no reason other than simple spite or to have a good laugh; they are wildly superstitious and at times unconscionably cruel. These and other characteristics tell of a light-minded, irrational people incapable of sober, independent thought. Given these behaviors and the absurd figures that serve as governors of Glupov—like Brudasty who has a music box for a head, or the governor who has a head full of truffles—Saltykov-Shchedrin's city emerges as a true theater of the grotesque. There is absolutely no spiritual life in town, as people are moved only by baser physical impulses and a philosophy of the grotesque.

In the Dostoevskian Glupov, the jocular and irrational mindset of people suggests similarities to *The History of a Town,* less for any particular details and more for the grotesque microcosm Dostoevsky recreates. Like Saltykov-Shchedrin's *The History of a Town,* Dostoevsky's novel is a chronicle of the life of a town under the rule of its governors. In a direct nod to the many mad governors of Glupov, the town's governor in *Demons* also loses his mind, seemingly unable to handle the chaos of postreform Russian society. The life

---

49. Dostoevsky, *Demons,* 319; 10:249.
50. Ibid.

of the town after Pyotr's arrival is defined by collective grotesque degradation fueled by nearly unconscious, animalistic, pleasure-seeking behavior.

There is a collective "destructive laughter" "symptomatic of Pyotr's growing hold over the town"[51] that has at its center a group of "sneerers and jeerers"[52] led by the buffoon Lyamshin. The individuals in the group are irreverent about behavioral norms and, like the citizens of Glupov, mock religious symbols; they degrade everything spiritual that is held sacred in the novel's beginnings. For instance, when a respectable bookseller comes into town selling gospels, Lyamshin and a young seminarian place pornographic photographs in her bag while pretending to buy gospels. The fact that a venerable older gentleman assists them by providing the aforementioned pictures underscores larger processes of grotesque degradation in *Demons*. The spirituality of the townspeople has eroded to the point that they are even incapable of showing any sympathy toward the corpse of a man who has committed suicide. Indeed, the complete collapse of the town's spiritual life is made manifest when the icon of the Nativity of the Mother of God, a token of the town's ancient spirituality, is degraded and debased, while the townspeople only display indifference and mockery in response. The liberated Fedka and Pyotr Stepanovich desecrate the icon by stealing its jewels and releasing a mouse inside the sacred space, which reenacts in miniature the grotesque animalism overtaking the town, as Pyotr's grotesque hybridity seems to rub off on everyone.

No one is immune to this thoughtlessness and longing for degradation, and everyone behaves as though possessed by grotesque hybrid selves that drive them to strange behaviors. In fact, the grotesque degradation of the town's spiritual life is pervasive and systemic to the point where even the supposedly pious show no spiritual values but embrace the material like everyone else. The same group of "sneerers and jeerers" pays a visit to the town's "blessed man and prophet" Semyon Yakovlevich,[53] who is perceived as a holy fool and an ascetic. Despite perceptions of him, however, Semyon is inappropriately attached to the material world, living with a merchant "in ease and comfort" and appropriating the charitable donations made to the church.[54] When the group arrives at his residence, Semyon is shown eating with gusto, similarly to Pyotr Stepanovich. In response to the sufferings of his visitors, he mocks and curses them, giving them pounds of sugar instead of providing spiritual wisdom.

---

51. Leatherbarrow, *A Devil's Vaudeville: The Demonic in Dostoevsky's Major Fiction,* 124.

52. Dostoevsky, *Demons,* 320; 10:250.

53. Ibid., 325; 10:254.

54. Ibid.

The profoundly grotesque worldview that overtakes the townspeople is illustrated most directly during the fete organized in honor of the governesses of the province. Instead of turning into the enlightening experience it was supposed to be, the fete serves as a battleground in which the abstract idealism of characters like the governor's wife, Yulia Mikhailovna, and Stepan Trofimovich collides with the grotesque materialism of the likes of Lyamshin and Liputin. Once the public arrives, their expectations that food will be served transform Yulia Mikhailovna's idealistic fete into a scene for grotesque debasement. As the chronicler explains, even before the fete, the norms in town are upended, as the "foremost people" suddenly "began listening to [trashy people], and became silent themselves, and some even chuckled along in a most disgraceful way."[55] A Bakhtinian carnivalesque upending of reality occurs as the lesser people, who appear like grotesque, animalistic hybrids because they only care about food and a good scandal, dominate the scene, while Karmazinov, Stepan Trofimovich, and Yulia Mikhailovna are ridiculed for their idealism. Instead of paying attention to the artistic parts of the program, everyone wants to know about the buffet, and they begin to swear once they learn that there is no food to be had.

By part 3 of *Demons* the narrative is transported from Varvara Petrovna stilted gentry drawing room from part 1 to the socially uncontrolled environment of the fete where everyone is given free rein and there is no room left for gentry decorum. All the narrative forces contained in part 1, like Captain Lebyadkin who offends and makes a scandal during the banquet, are released in part 3. As chaos takes over the narrative and characters perish one after another, the limitations of landowner literature in depictions of Russia after the Great Reforms also become apparent. By borrowing both elements of landowner literature and the anti-nihilist grotesque, Dostoevsky moves beyond conventional forms to capture the disorder of his contemporary Russia.

By the time Dostoevsky's *Demons* was published, a major transformation was in place in grotesque realism in Russian literature. Introduced into Russian belles lettres through the conservative anti-nihilist novel, and presented even earlier in left-leaning, non-novelistic works like Saltykov-Shchedrin's *The History of a Town,* the grotesque assumes a broader representational role in *Demons.* Previously aimed at outsiders like the nihilists, in *Demons* the grotesque extends to gentry characters like Nikolai Stavrogin. As a social outsider, Pyotr Stepanovich appears like an animalistic grotesque other, but Stavro-

---

55. Dostoevsky, *Demons,* 462; 10:354.

gin also cuts a monstrous figure. He does not live up to the role expected of him and proves no more than a shell of a man and facilitator of disorder and crime. Embodying the kind of character normally privileged in novels that Dostoevsky saw as exemplars of landowner literature, Stavrogin not only fails but disappears altogether, thus denoting the disintegration of the gentry protagonist. At least judging by his example, it is clear that Dostoevsky does not see the "beautiful order" of the gentry as something that can prevail in the chaos of postreform Russia. Instead of being a gentry hero who foils nihilist designs, Stavrogin is simply along for the ride with the "sneerers and jeerers" in town. All ideals crumble with him and his failure to attain moral nobility as a figure. As the townspeople engage in grotesque behavior, Stavrogin dies alone by his own hand, having failed to conjure any kind of moral community.

The decline of Stavrogin marks the beginnings of the grotesque as a style that captures the fall of the gentry in Russian literature. Stavrogin is, in a sense, the first in a genealogical line of monstrous gentry characters, grotesque hybrids dehumanized by their authors. As will be seen in chapters 4 and 5 of this book, both Saltykov-Shchedrin's *The Golovlev Family* and Tolstoy's *Resurrection* focus their aesthetic lenses on these monstrous gentry characters. By the time of Saltykov-Shchedrin's and Tolstoy's novels, the monstrous nihilist outsiders have left the scene, and the only remaining monsters are society's ultimate insiders, the gentry themselves. Indeed, in *Resurrection* a complete reversal of the original anti-nihilist model occurs, as the gentry appear monstrous whereas the revolutionaries are moral and upstanding characters.

Beyond the transformation of the gentry protagonist into a monster, Dostoevsky's *Demons* also transforms the novel form, rendering it into something more than a genre devoted to the gentry. But, interestingly, instead of doing this directly, Dostoevsky expands the novel form by refracting its previous model. In *Demons* the reader finds an estranged work of landowner literature that betrays the limitations of novels exclusively focused on the gentry lifestyle as the rest of Russia seethed in turmoil. In a sense, then, *Demons* sets the stage for *The Golovlev Family* and *Resurrection,* which present completely estranged forms of the realist novel, turning its tropes on their head in order to show the fall of the gentry. If, up until then, the novel had been detached from contemporary disorders and had reinforced the stability of the status quo by lionizing the gentry, then Dostoevsky stripped the genre of such protections. By subsuming the world of the novel into a grotesque microcosm, he could show what he believed to be the true face of Russian reality, complete with its ugliness and chaos.

CHAPTER 3

THE GENTRY HEROINE AS GROTESQUE OTHER

Roots of Tolstoy's Grotesque Aesthetic in *Anna Karenina*

Introduced into Russian realism through depictions of social outsiders like the nihilists and then redirected toward the gentry protagonist in *Demons*, grotesque realism extends to depictions of the female gentry heroine in the late 1870s with Tolstoy's *Anna Karenina*. As Irina Paperno points out, Tolstoy intended to have nihilists present at key junctures of the novel's plot but eventually decided to touch only indirectly on nihilist themes and the woman question.[1] In many respects, even though *Anna Karenina* does not directly capture a cohort of nihilists, the novel enters into broader dialogue with earlier anti-nihilist novels, including Dostoevsky's *Demons*, by continuing their aesthetic of grotesque realism. In *Anna Karenina*, just like in *Cathedral Folk, The Precipice,* and *Demons,* the grotesque is situated somewhere between death and sexuality, or the corpse and the animalistic, sexualized body. Tolstoy's eponymous heroine stands at the heart of the work's grotesque realism, bringing together in her plotline these different axes of desire, sexuality, and death.

Despite the great scholarly attention devoted to Anna Karenina and the inner division she experiences in the novel (between her passion for Vron-

---

1. Paperno, 154.

sky and her maternal love for Seryozha, among other such divisions), there have been relatively fewer treatments of the artistic devices Tolstoy employs to depict his heroine's inner split.[2] My focus in this chapter will be on how Anna's inner division is given artistic form by Tolstoy and how this split relates to the larger and complicated dichotomy he envisioned between the body and spirituality. Although *Anna Karenina* predates the moralistic style of the later Tolstoy with his predilection for naked didacticism, the novel is not without its tendentiousness,[3] and in tracing the grotesque in the narrative, we can also see how the style becomes an artistic forum for many of Tolstoy's later ideas, including those about the nature of the subject.

In his later theological writings, Tolstoy saw the human spirit as having a divine origin while he also cast the body as its earthly coffin that would perish as the soul returned to its divine source. In his view, those who lived their lives fixated on the body and bodily pleasures, and the attendant egocentric selfishness, would meet their inevitable end with that body. As I show, in *Anna Karenina* Tolstoy uses the grotesque to prefigure some elements of this important dialectic, relying on its aesthetic and philosophy of the body in order to demarcate the body-centered life. Anna, whose affair and sexual desire motivate much of the novel, is an important centerpiece for the style, which now moves from the male to the female gentry protagonist.

Beyond the heroine herself, the grotesque becomes instrumental in the depiction of minor characters, like Levin's dying brother, Nikolai, as well as other gentry characters. As in other works where death is often foregrounded through the grotesque, Tolstoy renders the death of Nikolai as the most physical and most grotesque act in the novel. As I argue, through his use of the grotesque that problematizes and extenuates the body, Tolstoy forges links between Nikolai's horrible death and Anna's affair. If, as Nikolai's agony reveals, death most directly binds us to our bodies, Anna's embrace of sexual passion during her affair similarly aligns her with the body and its inevitable demise. Over time, as she becomes immersed in her sexual desire, like Stavrogin, although she grows more and more beautiful, Anna comes to resemble a grotesque automaton.

As grotesque realism moves out of the nihilist genre and into the realist novel at large, we see it help launch larger questions in *Anna Karenina* about

---

2. See Alexandrov, *The Limits of Interpretation: The Meanings of Anna Karenina*, 198–201, 250–51; Mandelker, *Framing Anna Karenina: Tolstoy, the Woman Question, and the Victorian Novel*, 141–62.

3. In the words of Henry Gifford, in *Anna Karenina* Tolstoy manages to "combin[e] a wonderful candour with a highly tendentious design." Gifford and Williams, "D. H. Lawrence and Anna Karenina: An Exchange of Views," 99.

the place assigned to the body and bodily desire in gentry society. In *Anna Karenina* this world is not quite a microcosm for the grotesque, but we can observe considerable spiritual decay in the group. Moreover, the grotesque assumes a broader significance through its reverberations into Levin's story-line; it is only with the help of a peasant and an outsider to his own social sphere that Levin learns lessons contrary to the life of the body in his search for meaning.

I.   DEATH AND THE GROTESQUE IN *ANNA KARENINA*

The grotesque in Russian realism and in *Anna Karenina* in particular is deeply connected to bodily death and the image of the corpse. As a decomposing being drained of spiritual energy and no longer sentient, the corpse serves as a sort of center for the grotesque aesthetic in the Russian novel. In Tolstoy's fiction in particular, where we see plenty of beautiful and harmonious bodies that exude life and energy, the grotesque figures prominently in depictions of death. We can trace its roots as far back as Tolstoy's debut novella, *Childhood,* where Nikolenka's mother is depicted as a repulsive and terrifying *it* that is no longer human. Throughout the author's works, from the death of Pierre Bezukhov's father to the death of the old Prince Bolkonsky, where we see indi-viduals lose control of their dying bodies that move and spasm unconsciously, Tolstoy's depictions of corpses bring to light the grotesque aesthetic and serve as reminders of the dichotomy he envisioned between soul and body.

At its most extreme, this dichotomy is articulated in the theoretical writ-ings of Tolstoy's later years. In works like the *Harmonization and Translation of the Four New Testament Gospels* (1881), Tolstoy describes the relationship between body and soul as emerging from the union of God's immortal spirit or *"razumenie"* [comprehension] with the body born of human parents.[4] In a statement more radical than what we see in his art, Tolstoy compares the life of the body, particularly when this life centers on sexual pleasure, to ani-mal existence and death. Moral individuals who live for the spirit are godlike and able to access God's essence within their own spirits. Those who prefer to experience only the physical side of existence are trapped inside a dying shell—the body. "When we are born, our spirits are placed into the coffins of our bodies," declares Tolstoy in the later work *The Path of Life* (1910), cit-

---

4. All references pertain to the ninety-volume edition, Tolstoy, *Polnoe sobranie sochinenii, v 90 tomakh, akademicheskoe iubileinoe izdanie* (*PSS*). Unless otherwise indicated, all transla-tions are my own. Tolstoy, *Polnoe sobranie sochinenii,* 24:37.

ing Heraclitus.[5] "This coffin—our body—gradually deteriorates, and our soul is set free."[6] The body, which serves as the mortal shell of the spirit, is thus conceived as nothing more than an object. As Tolstoy suggests, through God, individuals can attain "non-temporal, indestructible life,"—a purely spiritual form of existence. Yet "by relying on . . . temporal life, believing in it, man is destroyed, dies."[7] "What we call earthly life is death," writes Tolstoy. "Today, tomorrow, it will come to an end."[8] Earthly life, especially when devoted to bodily pleasures like sex, emerges as a state of living death with the body as the sarcophagus of the soul. On the other hand, the life of the spirit that leads us back to a spiritual source, or God, grants a form of impersonal immortality once the "soul is set free" of its earthly coffin.

The hybridity between corpse and living human body that Tolstoy constructs in his later theoretical tracts powerfully evokes the grotesque as we see it in Russian realism. The author takes these ideas even further in the later essay, "On Life" (1887), where he discusses the life of the body by relying on the other spectrum of the grotesque: the hybridity between man and animal. Tolstoy describes two layers of human existence: the life of the self not grounded in time and space but connected to the spirit of God, and the personal life tied to time and space, synonymous with animal existence. "Man is born, the dog, the horse, are born, each has a special body," he writes.[9] "This body lives a certain time and then dies, decomposes, passes into other beings, and ceases to be. . . . The heart beats, the lungs act—the body does not decompose, the man, the dog, the horse live. The heart ceases to beat, respiration is arrested—the body begins to decompose; the animal is dead."[10] Although he does not call man an outright animal in this statement, through his intentionally reductive reasoning, Tolstoy equates a layer of human life to animal existence. In so doing, he violates the boundaries between man and animal and calls to mind the grotesque. Reduced to their flesh, human beings can appear as lower hypostases of themselves—a person can seem like an animal, a corpse, or an object-like being with little animation.

The grotesque rhetoric and strict separation between body and soul in Tolstoy's theoretical works had subtler, artistic, beginnings in Tolstoy's fiction, beginning even as early as *Anna Karenina*. Written shortly before the author's spiritual crisis that was precipitated by his deep fear of death, *Anna*

---

5. Ibid., 45:471
6. Ibid.
7. Ibid., 24:752.
8. Ibid., 24:531.
9. Ibid., 26:331–32.
10. Ibid.

Karenina is understandably bound up with Tolstoy's concerns about mortality. Although the novel lacks the monochromatic ideological messages of a later work like *Resurrection,* already in the depiction of Nikolai Levin's death, we see Tolstoy's terror and his simultaneously desperate effort to articulate a way out of death's finality. Scholars have noted this duality throughout his later works, some of which express confidence while others betray the author's persisting fear.[11] We can already see this model in *Anna Karenina* where the loophole out of death's finality rests in the dichotomy between body and spirit.

This larger metaphysical drama of mortality is played out aesthetically in Tolstoy's depiction of the death of Nikolai Levin—himself a member of the gentry at some point but essentially disowned by them due to his romantic misadventures—serves as an important instance of grotesque realism. Falling somewhere in between the nauseating corpse of the merchant that fouls the air in Tolstoy's later *Resurrection* and the completely decomposed, object-like body that appears in *Cathedral Folk,* Nikolai's body retains some of its fleshy essence while also withering away. Described as a part-human and part-object hybrid, the dying Nikolai is no longer a person but an objectified, blanket-covered thing—a monstrous other that hardly belongs to the human race. As Tolstoy homes in on the sick man, he repeatedly dehumanizes Nikolai, referring to him as just "the body,"[12] describing his "wasted limbs" incomprehensibly attached "to the long arm-bone," as well as the taut, as if transparent, forehead.[13] The narrator emphasizes the grotesquery of Nikolai's emaciated figure by showing various body parts jutting outwards, like "the long, white frame of his back, with enormous protruding shoulder blades, the ribs and vertebrae sticking out."[14]

As an aesthetic preoccupied with physicality and the degradation of the individual to the physical register, the grotesque becomes the means through which the life of the body, this purported mortal coffin of the immortal soul, is captured and separated from the soul in *Anna Karenina.* Tolstoy renders Nikolai's final moments in purely physical terms, emphasizing the bodily struggle in the process of dying. As he points out, Nikolai's body, the main protagonist in the scene, is overwhelmed by painful sensation. All processes involving the body, which up until then had felt natural and pleasurable, have

---

11. See Jahn's "Tolstoj's Vision of the Power of Death and 'How Much Land Does a Man Need?'" 442–53.

12. I will provide citations from the Pevear and Volokhonsky translation of *Anna Karenina* (New York: Penguin Books, 2000) first, and the citation from Tolstoy's original text will follow after a semicolon. *Anna Karenina,* 495; 19:64–65.

13. Ibid.

14. Ibid., 494; 19:63.

grown odious to the dying man. The body is not simply a coffin but also a chamber of torture, causing unspeakable anguish while also robbing Nikolai's soul of all hope with each new crisis. Due to the pain of dying, Nikolai is forced into a state of exclusively physical subsistence, just as those around him, including the narrator, focus all their attention on his body. It is only when the suffering seems to dissipate somewhat that we are told Nikolai feels hope and is able to function on a spiritual level. The rest of the time, his pain ensures that his whole existence is confined to the level of the body. With its freely dangling, uncontrolled arms, this body, at least through Levin's eyes, appears shattered, unable to sustain life and outside of Nikolai's control. In the process, the man himself emerges as no longer a human being, but as a grotesque inanimate object that more closely resembles corpses other than that of his brother Levin.

In his rendition of the dying man as a monstrous other, Tolstoy emphasizes the dichotomy between body and soul, making it clear that Nikolai's being and soul are not involved in the drama of dying. Tolstoy describes Nikolai's "living eyes," often full of hope, which are a window into a soul that remains alive.[15] It is only the body, this soul's grotesque temporal shell, that participates in the horrific process. This separation of body and soul in death calls to mind Tolstoy's later theoretical understanding of the body as a coffin for the spirit. As Tolstoy's writings reveal, over time he became very committed to the idea that the self could not be equivalent to the body but was rather anchored in the spirit which derived from God. At best, the body provided temporary shelter for the soul, and, at worst, it led the soul and true self astray through its physical naggings. "It cannot be that this terrible body is my brother Nikolai," thinks Konstantin Levin upon seeing his dying brother.[16] Levin has to see the "living eyes raised to him as he entered" and the "slight movement of the mouth under the matted moustache . . . to realize the terrible truth, that this dead body was his living brother."[17] Witnessing Nikolai's death, one cannot help agreeing with him that the essence of his brother, that part of him directly descended from God, or what Tolstoy would later call *razumenie,* cannot be the same as the shell of a body perishing from tuberculosis. Life and the self must surely come from elsewhere. "God is the God of the living, and not of the dead,"[18] says Jesus in Tolstoy's translation of the Gospel, thus emphasizing that only those who live for something greater that their bodily coffins can attain immortality in spirit.

---

15. Ibid., 491; 19:60.
16. Ibid.
17. Ibid.
18. Tolstoy, *PSS,* 24:752.

II. ANNA AS ARTISTIC OBJECT

If the body is the protagonist of Nikolai's drama, it is also the protagonist in the drama of Anna's affair. The relationship between body and soul in Anna spins out of balance when she consummates her relationship with Vronsky. Scholars have discussed the role that the force of sexuality assumes in Anna's life. Just as Nikolai's bodily suffering becomes his whole reality, so Anna's sexuality, or libido, becomes hers. R. P. Blackmur argues that Anna craves to "transmute what moves her from underneath—all that can be meant by libido, not sex alone—into personal, individual, independent love."[19] The libidinous energy that pushes Anna to leave everything for Vronsky and then wreck the relationship with him dominates her life to the point that this energy becomes an affliction no less than Nikolai's tuberculosis. The affliction of desire, much like that of tuberculosis, places the body at the center of Anna's life, a reorientation that becomes the basis from which we can read this life as fueled by the philosophy of the grotesque.

Paradoxically, the key to Anna's grotesquery is precisely her beauty. Before the affair with Vronsky, Anna's beauty is a natural, integrated element of her personality, revealing her inner spirit. As Kitty notices at the ball where Anna and Vronsky dance, Anna's whole beauty is "simple, natural, graceful"; it does not require elaborate outfits but "stand[s] out from what she w[ears]."[20] Fittingly, in the beginning of the book Anna does not pay much attention to her outfits but clothes herself inexpensively by altering old dresses.

Once she begins her affair with Vronsky, however, the dichotomy between body and soul so fundamental in Tolstoy's later theoretical thought can already be felt in *Anna Karenina* as the world begins to "go double in [Anna's] soul [v dushe ee vse nachinaet dvot'sya]"[21] This doubling hints at the disruption of Anna's integrated sense of self by her affair and her ensuing focus on sexual desire and the body. Like Nikolai, whose pain-ridden body pulsates at every nerve and demands attention while carrying out the excruciating process of dying, Anna's body radiates with desire and similarly commands attention. But if the body is the coffin of the soul, that part of the self condemned to death, in choosing to live for it, Anna is sharing in its death sentence. Indeed, judging by Tolstoy's language, her affair is no less violent than Nikolai's dying. In the couple's first postcoital scene, the adoring Vronsky covering Anna's body with kisses is compared to a murderer "cutting [his victim]

---

19. Blackmur, "Anna Karenina: The Dialectic of Incarnation," 434.
20. Tolstoy, 79; 18:84.
21. Ibid., 288; 18:305.

into pieces."[22] Vronsky does not actually murder Anna, but he sexualizes her body, and Tolstoy's implication is that this sexual relationship violates and lessens her psyche.

In this sense, Anna after the affair is depicted in a manner that closely resembles Tolstoy's depiction of the statuesque Helene Bezukhov from the earlier *War and Peace*. As someone who successfully navigates adultery, incest, and bigamy, Helene is obviously motivated by a powerful sensuality of her own, not dissimilar to the one Anna possesses. However, in Helene's case even more so than in Anna's, Tolstoy could not see female desire as compatible with spirituality. Helene turns into nothing more than a temptress, a siren, and a frozen statue of beauty. We are repeatedly told by Tolstoy and men who observe her, like Pierre Bezukhov, that she is utterly incapable of thoughts and feelings. She is just the ultimate object of male desire emptied of all individuality and spirituality. Anna is never emptied to this level, and it is perhaps her own unwillingness to exist like an empty vessel for desire that pushes her to suicide.

Judging by how these two female characters are depicted, and how the later character Maslova is also described as dead because of her constant sexual activity as a prostitute, we can observe a clear anxiety in Tolstoy's work where female erotic desire was concerned. For the most part, female characters do not seem able to retain much of their personalities while navigating erotic desire. It was one or the other—and the author was not diverging so profoundly from his earlier work in the later *Kreutzer Sonata* when he talked about how destructive male desire and mutual sexual consummation could be for women.

It is in these depictions that the grotesque serves as a helpful instrument for Tolstoy. In *Anna Karenina* the style helps illustrate how desire causes Anna to become estranged from herself. By the novel's end, there is the Anna we know from the beginning and then there is also the Anna possessed by her sexual desire, the Anna whose light-minded behavior and statue-like demeanor almost causes her to resemble Helene. The grotesque, present as more an idea and a philosophy than an aesthetic, emerges in this degradation of Anna's life to a body-centered existence where beauty is the only distinguishing trait. Broadly speaking, the grotesque realism traced here fluctuates on a spectrum from outright ugliness and animalism, as is the case with the Golovlevs, to automatized figures like the handsome Nikolai Stavrogin. Within this spectrum, Anna Karenina falls closer to Stavrogin with his mask-like face. Unlike Maslova, who becomes puffy and loses her beauty in her grotesque degrada-

---

22. Ibid., 149; 18:158.

tion and objectification, Anna grows more and more beautiful in the course
of her affair. But earlier on, this beauty is natural and seemingly effortless,
whereas after the affair, it seems profoundly unnatural and laboriously engi-
neered by some of the latest technological advances in fashion and medicine.

Anna dresses lavishly and expensively, going out of her way to enhance her
beauty with fashions from Paris, which emerge from the same industrial, and
in Tolstoy's opinion deeply dehumanizing, world of the railroad. The crinoline
made out of pure steel is mentioned in passing as the current fashion in Paris
during Levin and Kitty's wedding. Indeed, the demand for the crinoline was
so high that it even gave a boost to the steel industry.[23] Likewise, Anna relies
on birth control to maintain her figure, a late nineteenth-century medical
achievement that replaced abortion as the only means of avoiding unwanted
pregnancy.[24]

This deliberate construction of beauty fits with Amy Mandelker's suggestion that Anna's is not naturally beautiful but often schematized within a
frame of beauty and corporality that she cannot escape. She does not seem to
have an unvarnished self but seeks to present herself as an art object, an objet
d'art.[25] In assuming this object-like status, she becomes almost entirely outward oriented and strives to make herself into the object of all male desire and
fantasy. As one can observe from her conversations with the various males in
her household, like Svyazhevsky, Veselovsky, and others, her interactions are
predicated on her own attractiveness. She thus espouses the philosophy of
the grotesque in her reduction of everything to the level of physical beauty.
Instead of engaging ideas, she speaks and acts in such a way as to emphasize
her own loveliness or that of her hands and other body parts. Indeed, scholars
have noted that there is a repulsive undertone to Anna's astonishing beauty in
the novel. Vronsky, who is the main audience for this beauty, finds it irritating,
almost too lavish and audacious in its allure. As Mandelker puts it, Vronsky
finds Anna's beauty "empty and superficial" and "virtually pornographic."[26]
The reason that Mikhailov's painting is so effective is precisely that, as a form
of true art, it serves as a corrective copy, capturing Anna's soul and her original essence.

By becoming a perfect though inhuman artistic object, Anna experiences
deep alienation between her inner self, thus evoking the profound dichotomy

---

23. Goscilo, "Keeping A-Breast of the Waist-land: Women's Fashion in Early Nineteenth-
Century Russia," 51.

24. Barbara Engel discusses something known as a vaginal pessary, which women could
insert into their vaginal cavities themselves to prevent pregnancy. See *Mothers and Daughters:
Women of the Intelligentsia in Nineteenth-Century Russia*, 193.

25. Mandelker, 4.

26. Ibid., 118.

between flesh and spirit in Tolstoy. This alienation is perhaps most overtly expressed when Anna utters, "I don't know myself," on the way to the train station to take her own life.[27] Truly, in her effort to embrace libido and erotic love, and to preserve the dynamism of the original passion by remaining extraordinarily attractive to her partner, Anna seems completely estranged from herself. When it becomes clear that her love for Vronsky and her love for Seryozha cannot be reconciled, she increasingly suppresses her own spirituality and spiritual sorrow by narrowing her eyes in order to avoid seeing what she does not wish to see.

One obvious example of this emotional stultification and Anna's use of her beauty as a mask for her soul can be encountered during Dolly's visit to Vronsky's estate at Vozdvizhenskoe. As Dolly notices, Anna shows "superficial indifference" in conversation and keeps her feelings and innermost thoughts locked in an inner compartment inside her soul.[28] She only wants her interlocutor to observe the outward motions of her beautiful body. When Vronsky goes to speak to Anna after Dolly's departure, she again uses her beauty as a mask for her soul. "In her expression," writes Tolstoy from Vronsky's point of view, "excitedly restrained and concealing something, he found only that beauty which, familiar as it was, still captivated him, and her awareness of that beauty and her desire that it affect him."[29] Instead of delving into the problems of their relationship, Anna maintains her exclusive focus on her own body and believes Vronsky's curious look to be motivated by desire.

Despite Anna's beauty, her transformation into an object of art powerfully evokes the grotesque. Although Anna does not become a hollow marionette like the Korchagins from *Resurrection,* or animalistic like members of the Golovlev family, she loses substantial portions of her humanity through the affliction caused by her libido. The human in her gives way to the art object to the point that even the earthy Konstantin Levin observes that Anna's face seems to freeze up mid-conversation during their sole meeting. This same rigid quality of Anna's "frozen" face confronts Vronsky when he finds her body after the suicide.[30] As Mandelker suggests, in committing suicide, Anna simply completes the job of becoming a work of art.[31] Even lifeless, Anna's face remains beautiful, which only reinforces the extent to which her spirituality and real self are divorced from the frozen, doll-like beauty she so painstakingly creates throughout the novel. In becoming a frozen objet d'art, Anna's body is as divorced from her soul as Nikolai's withered body with rake-like

---

27. Tolstoy, 760; 19:340.
28. Ibid., 617; 19:192.
29. Ibid., 641; 19:218.
30. Ibid., 780; 19:362.
31. Mandelker, 104.

hands. In both cases, the individual becomes a hybrid, part-human and part-object grotesque creature.

In fact, one might argue that Anna bears some indirect resemblance to E. T. A. Hoffman's automatized woman, Olympia. With a striking figure and face, yet terribly stiff in her personality with hollow eyes and hands as cold as ice, Olympia is the essential aesthetic object; she is compared to a statue, and looking at her makes the protagonist, Nathaniel, think about eternal beauty. As a female machine, Olympia also touches on a quintessential male fantasy: she is the perfect female love machine. In her obsession with beauty, male desire, and the narrowing of her eyes, Anna seeks to degrade herself to level of a beautiful object, no different from Olympia. Although there is no place for the actual human machine within the bounds of the realist novel, Anna's objecthood and her hybridity between the human and the statue become apparent more subtly and fleetingly.

III. DEGRADING OTHERS

Thinking of the importance that Anna assigns the body and all the ways in which she is dehumanized due either to her fixation with physical beauty or to the pressures of maintaining that beauty, it is worth noting that this body-centric perspective also defines how she sees others. For instance, partly due to her own guilt about what she has done to him, Anna regularly objectifies Karenin in her perception. Multiple times in the novel, she describes him as something inhuman and cannot bring herself to imagine that he could be genuinely suffering as a result of her actions. In Anna's eyes, Karenin is not a man; "he is a machine [mashina], a wicked machine when he gets angry."[32] A bit later, she refers to him as a "puppet"[33] and an "administrative machine."[34] In Anna's eyes, Karenin is no longer a human being but rather a grotesque thing, a hybrid between man and object. She shudders when she also notices his ugliness at other times, like when she sees his large ears at the novel's beginning, or toward the end when she thinks about his swollen veins and cracking fingers. Anna's dehumanization of her husband to the level of a grotesque puppet and a machine is aimed at justifying her own immoral behavior through aesthetics. How can the beautiful Anna not cheat on the grotesque and unattractive Karenin?

---

32. Tolstoy, 189; 18:199.
33. Ibid., 360; 18:379.
34. Ibid.

Aside from dehumanizing Karenin, as Anna gets closer to the final act of her life, her suicide, she begins to view everyone around her as profoundly grotesque. She sees young men with "ugly, insolent impressions" and "an ugly lady with a bustle," and she even finds a little girl to be "ugly and affected."[35] As her own spirituality slips away from her, Anna projects a grotesque, dehumanizing look on the world, as Tolstoy frequently employs the Russian word "*urodlivyi*" [ugly] in describing the world from her perspective.

Naturally, this kind of body-centric, grotesque reasoning also leads to profound isolationism. Confined to his aching body, the dying Nikolai must contend with his every aching nerve and begins to resent everyone else for not experiencing the torment that so plagues his final hours. Anna similarly finds herself in a state of total alienation from the world. Consumed by her bodily desires and the jealousy that they provoke, she feels that everyone is at odds with everyone else. "Aren't we all thrown into the world only in order to hate each other and so to torment ourselves and others?" she says on her way to her final journey.[36] She feels that the world is driven by Yashvin's principles of "struggle for existence and hatred" and finds that she even hates Vronsky all the while loving him.[37] As Maire Kurrik argues, the body becomes not an "opening" for her . . . but a source of disrelatedness, of lovelessness, solitude, and the ugly, meaningless, particularity of things."[38] Indeed, while Anna is surrounded by people, her suicide is as lonely as Stavrogin's suicide in the attic at Skovoreshniki. Stavrogin dies alone, having become an outcast instead of a communal leader, just as Anna and Nikolai similarly die alone, engulfed in their bodily isolation.

Even though *Anna Karenina* is not overtly political and even though in *Demons* Dostoevsky amends the original politics of the anti-nihilist novel by enveloping the gentry protagonist into the grotesque, we still see traces of the original isolation of the grotesque dating back to the anti-nihilist novel. Although Bakhtin describes the grotesque and bodily life as defined by communal jubilation, many nineteenth-century works of grotesque realism show this togetherness as altogether missing. In the anti-nihilist novel, the grotesque marked nihilists as different and as monstrous outsiders, thus reinforcing their status as social outsiders. Even as the monsters grew normalized and became members of traditional social groups, the grotesque remained a style of isolation, as a body-centric life was deemed a barrier to togetherness. Indeed, like Solovev and others, Tolstoy, often saw bodies as shells separating individuals

---

35. Ibid., 765; 19:344.
36. Ibid., 764; 19:342.
37. Ibid., 762; 19:338.
38. Maire Kurrik, *Literature and Negation*, 126.

from one another. In his later work, he would deem the life of the soul, a life marking the divine beginnings of humanity and common to all people, as the kind of existence that could join individuals into spiritual togetherness.

IV. THE GROTESQUE AND THE LARGER GENTRY MILIEU

The question of the rapport between body, soul, desire, isolation, and community, although not as crudely expressed in *Anna Karenina* as in Tolstoy's later fiction, are already relevant in this work. The tensions between living the life of the body versus living a moral existence are treated in the novel as a whole, and they spill from Anna's plotline to Levin's. Although Levin does not experience the detachment from himself that Anna or the dying Nikolai do, he too is confronted with some of the questions that confront her and that evoke the grotesque in the novel.

In particular, after his son's birth and his brother's death, in part 8 of the novel, Levin undergoes a spiritual crisis similar to the one Tolstoy himself underwent. He starts to think about death and its inevitability—and how it will erase any meaning constructed in human life. Equating his life on earth to the existence of a bubble that "holds out for a while and then bursts," Levin feels dejected and desperately seeks a higher meaning or explanation behind it all.[39] "Without knowing what I am and why I'm here I cannot live," thinks Levin, all the while feeling that he cannot know the answers to these questions.[40] Like Tolstoy, he embarks on a series of philosophical inquiries into these questions, until finally he discovers his answer in the simplest place, with the peasant Fyodor. Fyodor tells Levin about the peasant Platon who is willing to help others instead of seeking profit. This willingness to help others at a cost to himself is described by Fyodor as the equivalent of living for spirit and remembering God, whereas a life of selfish gain is seen as living for the flesh.

The struggle within Levin bears similarities to the struggle within Anna, but while she can only choose the body, Levin follows Platon in choosing the spirit over the flesh. Interestingly, while for Anna the choice of the body means total alienation from others, for Levin the choice of the spirit means living one's life through the principle of love for others. As much as loving everyone proves more of a struggle in practice than in theory, at the end of the novel Levin is committed to the struggle. His efforts to attain this active

---

39. Tolstoy, 788; 19:370.
40. Ibid.

loving with others, as well as the argument that through love one can achieve a higher degree of meaning, provide a way to overcome the terror of death.

The struggle between body and soul in the novel, Anna's struggle with the body, her capitulation to its drives, and Levin's choice of the spirit, all look ahead to the body-soul dialectics in Tolstoy's later theoretical writings. In his translation of the New Testament Gospels, only a few short years after *Anna Karenina*, Tolstoy paid particular attention to this tension, re-envisioning it as one of the temptations of Christ. Tolstoy transforms the Satan's wilderness temptations of Christ into the "most common expression of an inner struggle [vnutrennayaya borba] which is repeated in the soul of every man."[41] He sees this struggle as between two "diametrically opposed principles of life [osnov zhizni]"—"asceticism" and "materialism."[42] Of course Jesus chooses the soul rather than the body. As Tolstoy articulates in the Gospel, "The true life [of the spirit] is the life which is common to all men." On the other hand, "The personal life is a deception of the flesh."[43] The body, which fuels the grotesque in *Anna Karenina,* is thus deemed a dividing force: those who live for the body die as individual bodies, while those who want to live for the spirit can share a common spiritual afterlife with other spirits in what Tolstoy describes as a "tree of life."[44]

Although there is no such strict binary between body and soul in the more sophisticated *Anna Karenina,* we can already note the tensions between the body and its drives and a more spiritual and morality-driven life. Most individuals, especially those inhabiting the gentry milieu, choose the body over the spirit. It is not surprising that Levin has to step out of his gentry world in order to find answers to his existential dilemma through the peasant Platon, whose example grants the message of love that no one in gentry society extends to Anna.

Although gentry society is not shown as thoroughly grotesque or as having succumbed to total spiritual collapse, if we think about it at large, we can nonetheless see considerable moral decay. Tolstoy does not paint gentry society with broad, grotesque brushes as he does in *Resurrection,* but through characters like Princess Betsy, Stiva Oblonsky, and other members of the gentry, he reveals the beginnings of the moral decline so vociferously decried in *Resurrection.*

When Stiva goes to St. Petersburg by the end of the novel, he is appalled at the immorality he encounters there. The city's gentry society seems completely

41. Tolstoy, 24:78.
42. Ibid., 24:80.
43. Ibid., 24:177.
44. Ibid., 24:755.

out of keeping with nature or morality. Children are considered a nuisance; everyone has affairs, or they live on borrowed money. His own loose morals notwithstanding, Stiva seems almost frightened at the erotic energy coming from someone like Princess Betsy or even Countess Lydia, despite her seeming piousness.

In fact, in many ways, Countess Lydia embodies the gentry's moral degradation that Tolstoy also renders through the grotesque. Described by Tolstoy as a yellow, unattractive, and aging woman desperately trying to conceal her unshapely and grotesque body through the most fashionable form-fitting outfits, the countess regularly speaks of Christian love. Yet as Tolstoy so clearly reveals, she tarnishes the very idea in her behavior toward Anna and immoral attachments to Karenin and other men. Whatever she may preach, Countess Lydia is ultimately attached to the life of the body and divisiveness. Indeed, although Anna espouses a philosophy of divisiveness at the end of the novel, one might argue that it is the mass rejection she experiences in society that ultimately forces her into her complete and utter isolation that becomes a self-fulfilling prophecy. As a social outcast, Anna cannot know any better and does not have any other options.

Written in the late 1870s, *Anna Karenina* echoes the deep fin-de-siècle pessimism that overwhelmed Europe around this same time. The novel also reverberates with explicitly Russian anxieties about the fate of the gentry. Even as the novel ends with Levin's life rather than Anna's death, one can sense great anxiety about the fate of Russia and Russian gentry in the face of the shifting realities of progress and industrialization in the late nineteenth century. In an essay about the beginning of *Anna Karenina,* Robert Louis Jackson argues that the adultery crisis in the Oblonsky home, just like the corpse found under the train, are not only references to Anna's death and destruction but also harbingers of the general "family, social and economic breakdown in Russian life."[45] Although Anna's desire is what directly wrecks her family life, throughout the novel Tolstoy also presents technology as an important force behind her collapse and a broader collapse among the gentry. Anna's tragedy begins at a visit to a train station, and later she chooses suicide under a train when she could perhaps use morphine to take her life. Her gruesome death and the likely impending casualties of the Russian soldiers going to fight the Turks present modernity and industrialization as violent forces in postreform Russia.

---

45. Jackson, "On the Ambivalent Beginning of Anna Karenina," 350–51.

Levin, a reliable mouthpiece for Tolstoy, repudiates technology, and, like the author, feels deeply uncomfortable and drowsy inside trains.[46] Besides the railroad, which is the most obvious form of technology in the novel, Levin also renounces agricultural technology, which Vronsky embraces wholeheartedly. As Levin insists, agriculture should rest on the relationship between the landowner and the worker, a fundamentally feudal bond predating the 1861 Emancipation. As critics have argued, Tolstoy had a surprisingly conservative attitude about the emancipation of the serfs, which he did not see as necessarily improving the lot of the peasants who at times shared nearly familial attachment with the gentry.[47] The few mentions of the time from before the emancipation, such as when Anna remembers driving on a carriage, suggest a purer and less technological reality. On the other hand, the railroad seems like a token of postreform Russia where, if they have a ticket, anyone can inhabit the same space despite any estate separations.

In *Anna Karenina* it is clear that the emancipation has in some ways also alienated the essential relationship between peasants and landowners, while also opening up opportunities for a new kind of relationship. When Levin mows with the peasants or when he learns about the peasant Platon who cares about the spirit, one is reminded of the deeper, pre-emancipation tie between the gentry and the peasants. By having a peasant help Levin through his journey, Tolstoy restores and indirectly improves this fundamental bond, which perhaps also constitutes the only possibility for renewal among the gentry. The gentry can retain their spirituality and humanity through close communion with peasants whose moral compass appears much more intact in Tolstoy's universe. After all, it is through his ties with the peasants that Levin learns lessons contrary to the life of the body and egoism that land Anna under the train.

Tolstoy's use of grotesque realism in *Anna Karenina* constitutes a crucial point in the Russian realist tradition. Although Levin manages to save himself by communing with the folk spirituality of the peasants, it is also clear that he is one of the few who are able to do so. Postreform Russia, just like the ominous trains we witness in *Anna Karenina,* seems to be moving much too fast. The overall moral decline among the gentry, although not always overtly depicted through the grotesque, foretells the grotesque rot in Mikhail Saltykov-Shchedrin's *The Golovlev Family.* By the time Saltykov-Shchedrin writes his novel, we notice a broadening of the grotesque, from a single hero (*Demons*) or heroine (*Anna Karenina*) to an entire microcosm.

46. See Jahn, "The Image of the Railroad in *Anna Karenina,*" 5.

47. See Anne Hrushka, "Love and Slavery: Serfdom, Emancipation, and Family in Tolstoy's Fiction," 627–46.

CHAPTER 4

GROTESQUE REALISM AND THE DECLINE OF THE GENTRY IN M. SALTYKOV-SHCHEDRIN'S *THE GOLOVLEV FAMILY*

The publication of *Anna Karenina,* a significant event in Russian literary circles, made a particularly strong impression on Mikhail Saltykov-Shchedrin. In an 1875 letter to Pavel Annenkov, Saltykov-Shchedrin referred to it as a "bovine novel" ("korov'ego romana"), much too focused on matters of the "genitalia" (detor [odnykh] chastei).[1] These indelicate and exaggerated comments, which perhaps also hint at the grotesque elements of *Anna Karenina,* were likely a response to what Saltykov-Shchedrin perceived as the frustratingly apolitical nature of the Russian novel. Despite their opposing political affiliations, Saltykov-Shchedrin, like Dostoevsky,[2] believed that with its predilection for gentry characters and spaces, the realist novel was out of touch with the turbulence of postreform Russia. In the series of essays and sketches published under the rubric *Gentlemen from Tashkent* (*Gospoda "Tashkentsy,"* 1869–72), Saltykov-Shchedrin argues that the "novel has lost its former basis, since the family and everything connected with it has begun to change in

---

1. Saltykov-Shchedrin, *Sobranie sochinenii v 20-ti tomakh,* 18; 2:180.

2. As I. B. Pavlova argues, Saltykov-Shchedrin shared the opinions on landowner literature as expressed in Dostoevsky's *The Adolescent.* See Pavlova, *Tema sem'i i roda u Saltykov-Shchedrina v literaturnom kontekste epokhi,* 117.

character."[3] *Anna Karenina* may have simply been the last straw in this overall growing distaste for the genre. Like Dostoevsky, Saltykov-Shchedrin also took matters into his own hands by publishing a sketch titled "Family Court" in *Notes of the Fatherland*. Over time, this narrative grew into what we know as *The Golovlev Family* (*Gospoda golovlevy*, 1875–80), a work with all the appearances of a family novel.

Appearances could be deceiving, however, as the family novel facade in *The Golovlev Family* only underscores the downfall of the gentry family. Called a "long obituary" by one critic, *The Golovlev Family* narrates the decay of the gentry family from one generation to the next, showing lives marked by failure, immorality, and eventually death.[4] In capturing this decline, Saltykov-Shchedrin also makes more broad use of grotesque realism. In his hands, the style no longer captures segregated characters but expands to the whole world of the novel, becoming the lens through which the author recounts the gentry downfall.

In particular, Saltykov-Shchedrin uses grotesque realism to envelop and distort the traditional gentry narrative as pioneered by Sergei Aksakov in *Family Chronicle* (*Semeinaya khronika*, 1856). A "model . . . in terms of both content and form, to the family novels of Turgenev, Goncharov, and especially Tolstoi,"[5] Aksakov's *Family Chronicle* extolled and set high expectations for the gentry and their lives. Despite the major differences in content, critics have noted the thematic and formal similarities between *The Golovlev Family* and *Family Chronicle*, describing Saltykov-Shchedrin's novel as "a near perfect mirror image" that completely inverts Aksakov's earlier narrative.[6] As I argue, this transformation of the earlier narrative happens through the grotesque. Saltykov-Shchedrin relies on the style to distort familiar motifs of gentry life in the countryside and replace them with a warped narrative about a family that looks the same as any family from the outside, but has undergone spiritual and moral collapse.

Aksakov's *Family Chronicle* showed family life as shaped by four staple elements: the figure of the landowner, the aura of stability on the gentry estate, daily food rituals, and, finally, the well-developed psychological landscape of gentry characters. Through the broken and destructive Golovlevs, Saltykov-Shchedrin undermined all of these elements of earlier gentry narratives. In *The Golovlev Family* the landowner is turned into a hollow and animalistic

---

3. Quoted in Kramer, 124.

4. Quoted in Foote, "Saltykov and the Golovlyovs," 7.

5. Durkin, *Sergei Aksakov and Russian Pastoral*, 244.

6. Todd, "The Anti-Hero with a Thousand Faces: Saltykov-Shchedrin's Porfiry Golovlev," 102.

shell stripped of his or her humanity, degraded to the level of coarse food consumption. Along with the person of the landowner, the entire gentry manor also turns into a stagnant, grotesque microcosm equivalent to a tomb.

I. THE TRADITIONAL IMAGE OF THE LANDOWNER AND THE GENTRY MICROCOSM

Despite his inveterate leftist leanings, at least biographically Saltykov-Shchedrin was as much of a landowner writer as Dostoevsky considered Tolstoy or Turgenev to be. A member of a wealthy provincial family, which could be considered old nobility with marriage ties going as far back as the family of Peter the Great, Saltykov-Shchedrin was intimately familiar with the figure of the Russian landowner. Indeed, it has been suggested that the figure of Arina Golovleva is based on the author's own mother, Olga.[7] This personal background might certainly account for Saltykov-Shchedrin's significant attention to the fate of the gentry in *The Golovlev Family*. If the first hints of grotesque realism as a broader gentry phenomenon first occur in *Anna Karenina*, they develop even further in *The Golovlev Family*, where we witness a larger characterization of the group as grotesque.

Beyond the biographical register, the other significant motivation for the Golovlev narrative of collective gentry decay was also the earlier valorization of the landowner role in Russian literature and society. The notion that being a good landowner was an honorable position can be traced as far back as the beginning of the nineteenth century or even earlier in Russian culture.[8] In the 1803 "Letter of a Country Dweller," Karamzin describes the landowner role as honorable, unapologetically declaring, "The main right of the Russian nobleman is to be a landowner, his main duty to be a good landowner; whoever fulfills this duty is serving his fatherland as a faithful son."[9] Before the emancipation of the serfs in particular, being a landowner was equated with a productive and honorable life; caring for as many as 800 or 1,000 serfs was deemed a greater service to the country than work in most professions. Major Russian authors, like Pushkin, Gogol, Aksakov, Turgenev, and Tolstoy,

---

7. Proffer, ix.

8. The significance of the Russian landowner can be traced back to the eighteenth century. Specifically, the role acquired greater cultural value after the gentry were freed from government service in 1762. For more on earlier conceptualizations of the landowner role, see Newlin, *The Voice in the Garden: Andrei Bolotov and the Anxieties of the Russian Pastoral*. See also Grigoryan.

9. Quoted in Newlin, 86.

advanced similar arguments in both their fiction and nonfiction, encouraging members of the gentry to embrace the role of landowner.

The treatment of the gentry in *The Golovlev Family* is deeply influenced by these previous narratives of gentry life, which help shape Saltykov-Shchedrin's grotesque realism. Many of the conventions of gentry literature, refracted in Saltykov-Shchedrin's later novel, were most prominently articulated in Sergei Aksakov's *Family Chronicle*, a work that was seen as the "*Aeneid* of Russian conservatism"[10] and that served as an ur-narrative for the Russian gentry family novel. Aksakov's created a myth of the gentry landowner that exalted the group and set high expectations for them. In his narrative, we encounter the beginnings of the very phenomenon that Dostoevsky decried when he protested against Russian landowner literature—the myth of gentry moral superiority later unraveled in Russian grotesque realism.

With "unusually wide shoulders, veined hands, hard, muscular body,"[11] Aksakov's Stepan Bagrov is a force of nature, a "heroic Patriarch"[12] who moves his family from Simbirsk to Ufa and domesticates the natural wild to build a comfortable nest. Bagrov uses his physical prowess to enclose the land, start up an agricultural enterprise, and provide shelter for the peasants; he undertakes seemingly heroic feats such as the founding of a mill and the construction of a dam for the river. As these acts reveal, Bagrov is completely in charge of his estate. When he is in good spirits, his infectious joy brightens up the household. Alternatively, the whole house quakes when he is angry: "That kind, virtuous and even lenient man sometimes darkened with such outbursts of rage," writes the narrator.[13] These outbursts sometimes result in violence against his wife and daughters, although, most of the time, Bagrov is kind and invested in his family's well-being.

The importance assigned to the landowner role in *The Golovlev Family* has its roots in Aksakov's chronicle. The heroic patriarch Bagrov is obsessed with his genealogy and belonging to the landowner class. In his youth he did not marry a woman he loved because there was a serf among her ancestors. Later, it is the skills of Kurolesov—the husband of Praskovia, Bagrov's cousin—as a landowner that blind Bagrov to the former's cruelty and inhumanity. Being a landowner is thus treated as a role of fundamental importance in *Family Chronicle*, perhaps touching on what Bella Grigoryan identifies as the ideal of the landowner-citizen during Catherine the Great's era and in the early decades of the nineteenth century. During this time, the landowner was seen

---

10. Todd, "The Anti-Hero with a Thousand Faces," 102.

11. Aksakov, *Sobranie sochinenii,* 1:76.

12. Todd, 102.

13. Aksakov, 1:89.

not as "a private autonomous creature, but as an individual with a job, a patri-otic citizen who serves the polity through the administration of his provincial property."[14]

Aside from the substantial managerial and civic roles that the landowner was meant to assume, he or she also had to take on important emotional roles as keeper of the family. Through the character of Bagrov, Aksakov con-structs a wholesome image of the landowner as both business manager of the estate and family caretaker.[15] However important his role as landowner, Bagrov pays as much attention to his role as father, exuding warmth and protecting family members at all times, while instinctively knowing when to bend his strict views for their sake. For instance, despite his initial qualms, he agrees to his son's marriage to Sofia and emerges as her protector against jealous sisters-in-law.

The kind of estate microcosm that results from Bagrov's stewardship is also worth discussing because it serves as a foundation for the grotesque microcosm we find in Saltykov-Shchedrin's *The Golovlev Family*. Aksakov's Bagrovo is a "closed and stable world," a microcosm made up of its own rou-tines and rituals that offer the "ideal of traditional life."[16] Bagrov has an estab-lished routine of repetitive actions: he wakes up, takes his tea, eats meals, inspects the estate, and participates in other similar activities. Indeed, aside from these family rituals, we can note that virtually everything that happens in Aksakov's Bagrovo is a repetition of past actions, thus lending the chronicle an aura of mythical cyclicality that protects it from history and linear histori-cal change. Historical events, like the Pugachev rebellion, take place virtually unnoticed and are mentioned only in passing. Within the sphere of Bagrovo, Aksakov permits only ritualistic actions that maintain an "unchanging equi-librium of man and his environment."[17] Outsiders like Kurolesov or Sofia are either defeated and cast out or integrated into the Bagrovo reality, so that despite occasional flare-ups, estate life is never disturbed for long.

Raised in a quiet corner of gentry life, the Bagrovs possess a steadiness and calm that seemingly stem directly from nature. Aleksei Bagrov has a pro-found connection to nature, which provides psychological stability and calm. This connection to nature renders Aleksei emotionally healthy and protects

14. Grigoryan, 25.

15. The figure of Bagrov was based on Aksakov's own grandfather, but as Andrew Durkin points out, Aksakov did not merely record the behaviors and character traits of real people in *Family Chronicle*. Rather, individuals in the work are "paradoxically both literary figures and actual people"; their characteristics contain shades of art and fictionalization, as well as innate traits, of the universal and of the particular (Durkin, 102).

16. Durkin, 120.

17. Ibid., 121.

him from some of the darker, hysterical impulses that plague his wife Sofia. She may not understand his love for nature and views it as pedestrian, but the narrator implies that this love gives Aleksei the ability to transcend what haunts others. He does not have the enterprising and strong character of his father, but he manages to attain inner psychic equilibrium, which the narrator describes as a positive character trait.

Aleksei and the many other gentry landowner protagonists that follow on the pages of Russian novels authored by Tolstoy, Turgenev, and others were also equipped with an inner world full of conflicting psychological traits and drives. The complex gentry psychology reflected in both Aleksei's depth and occasional passivity and his father's tempestuous yet ultimately tender personality was an elusive but pivotal feature of the gentry family narrative as it developed in Russian literature. When he recreates the gentry microcosm in *The Golovlev Family*, Saltykov-Shchedrin reacts against the gentry position, their world, and their psychology. Just as the gentry had been at the center of the Russian novel, so Saltykov-Shchedrin placed them at the heart of his novel, but he transformed them into monstrous versions of who they had been. Through grotesque realism, Saltykov-Shchedrin turned traditional gentry narratives on their head, using them to articulate a message of decline. Not only are the Golovlevs poor landowners who turn their estate into a tomb-like space, but they also appear as primitive beings without much psychological depth.

II. THE LANDOWNER TURNED INTO GROTESQUE AUTOMATON

The role of the landowner in gentry family narratives like Aksakov's *Family Chronicle* is purposefully recreated and greatly distorted in Saltykov-Shchedrin's *The Golovlev Family*. The novel begins with the image of Arina Golovleva, a major landowner in her region, at the height of her power prior to the 1861 Emancipation. Arina possesses nearly inexorable energy, single-handedly expanding the Golovlev fortune tenfold. "Thanks to her personal energy," writes the narrator, "this woman had raised the family to its highest-ever level of prosperity."[18] Her skill as landowner is born of a forceful and downright domineering personality that Saltykov-Shchedrin makes apparent. As we learn at the beginning of the novel, when a furious Arina retreats to her private study, "v dome vse vdrug smolklo, slovno umerlo" [the whole house

---

18. Saltykov-Shchedrin, 18:252.

suddenly [grows] silent, as if it had died].[19] Not only the servants but also her children are terrified of Arina, wondering, before undertaking any venture, how she will react to their actions.

As this brief introduction to Arina reveals, she privileges the role of landowner over that of parent and family guardian. In fact, the unbalanced rapport between these two capacities initially accounts for elements of the grotesque in Arina. She inherits Bagrov's energy and enterprising spirit as well as his tempestuous anger but has none of his warmth and only inspires fear in her family. She may have the same first name as Bagrov's wife, Arina Vasilevna Bagrova, described as "byla zhenshchina dobraya i ochen' prostaya" [a good and simple woman],[20] but the transformation of the mother figure into matriarch in *The Golovlev Family* results in a flourishing estate and a languishing family unit. Bagrov's occasional cruelty is present and greatly magnified in Arina who usually feels only anger toward family members. "She [Arina Golovleva] had too independent, or one might say too spinsterish, a nature [slishkom nezavisimaya, tak skazat', kholodnaya natura]," writes Saltykov-Shchedrin's narrator, "to see her children as anything other than a burden [obuzy]. She only breathed freely when she was left alone with her business accounts and plans, or when no one interrupted her discussions with estate managers, village elders, housekeepers, and others."[21] Arina amasses great wealth in the name of her family, all the while depriving her children of any kind of maternal affection.

In the image of Arina and of Porfiry, Bagrov is emptied of his humanity and spirituality and guided exclusively by landowner principles. Although we know that she is capable of emotional depth, Arina and, later, Porfiry usually allow empty clichés or entrepreneurial principles to take the place of ethical and spiritual consideration. To the detriment of the family unit, Arina relies exclusively on economic principles in her familial relationships, defining "her sole maternal responsibility in the callous terminology of an uneven business transaction."[22] We are told that she "derzhala detei vprogolod'" [kept her children half-starving] and fed her granddaughters, Anninka and Lyubinka, sour milk "for the sake of economizing."[23]

This strict abidance to financial principles results in the complete dehumanization of family members, reducing them to objects, or simply another

---

19. Ibid., 18:18.

20. Aksakov, 1:83.

21. Saltykov-Shchedrin, 18:13.

22. Kaminer, "A Mother's Land: Arina Petrovna Golovleva and the Economic Restructuring of the Golovlev Family," 551.

23. Saltykov-Shchedrin, 18:11.

part of her landowner's duties and patrimony. Although she partly redeems herself with the orphans and the second generation of Golovlevs, over time the grotesque mentality Arina applies to others comes to be reflected in her. In particular, Arina completely unravels when the social structure grows looser after the emancipation of the serfs. She splits the ownership of the Golovlev estate between her two sons, Porfiry and Pavel, thus ostensibly giving up the role of landowner herself. After spending her life privileging this role over every other role in life, she declines when she loses her estate and even the two orphan girls leave her.

In a searing portrayal of old age and senility, Saltykov-Shchedrin shows Arina reduced to a dazed and defenseless old woman—a grotesque empty being that only cares about tasty food. For the sake of her semi-animalistic appetites, she even makes amends with Porfiry in order to have access to Golovlevo's rich food preserves. The aging Arina, who has lived a life of work and privation, comes to conceptualize the good life as made up of "tasty tidbit[s]" [khoroshii kusok].[24]

The transformation of the strong-willed enterprising landowner into a grotesque shallow creature once she can no longer be a landowner suggests that the Great Reforms either produced or rendered more visible a decline among the gentry. In discussing the fate of the Golovlevs, Saltykov-Shchedrin's narrator holds that a "grim fate" hands over "lesser gentry families, which are scattered the length and breadth of Russia, without any links with the general life of the community, or any ruling sense."[25] As he notes, these small gentry families used to "take shelter behind serfdom"[26] but no longer have that protection since the Emancipation.

The alien and monstrous nature of the Golovlevs is most directly exposed in the person of Porfiry who defines the post-Emancipation generation of Golovlev landowners. Once he usurps Arina's role to become the family patriarch, one witnesses the same devotion to the empty role of landowner, to the point that Porfiry seems like a complete automaton and slave to these principles. Bakhtin cites the image of the soulless but still moving marionette as an important trademark of the grotesque. As he argues, artistic representations of the marionette focus on the "puppet as the victim of alien, inhuman force, which rules over men by turning them into marionettes."[27] Porfiry stands a marionette moved about by empty clichés, a puppet and a grotesque double of

---

24. Ibid., 18:98.
25. Ibid., 18:250.
26. Ibid., 18:250.
27. Bakhtin, *Rabelais*, 40.

Bagrov, who ultimately does not allow traditions to supplant his personhood or his parental impulses.

Like his mother, Porfiry adopts landowner and bureaucratic principles with his children and allows his three sons to perish due to parental indifference. Looking for new ways to expand his property, he cheats and bullies those around him with his endless and empty chatter. As William Mills Todd III argues, if Bagrov "fully realizes the heroic possibilities of the Russian estate, which permitted the landowner to perfect himself, reform his territories (socially and economically), and achieve a sort of pastoral utopia," then the ridiculous Porfiry is a travesty of all this.[28] Porfiry is driven exclusively by principles of accumulation and, until his own death, is deprived of all spiritual energies.

As testimony to the degeneration of the gentry generations,[29] Porfiry is considerably more dehumanized than Arina, who still retains some modicum of spirituality. Porfiry is so caught up in routine and empty aphorisms that we might see him as a domesticated version of Governor Brudasty with a music box for a head from Saltykov-Shchedrin's *History of a Town*. A creature of routine, Porfiry eats meals, has requiems sung, prays before icons, and engages in a web of idle talk and calculations. We are told that he is so deprived of spirituality and humanity that he could not even fit into the "v mertvom dele byurokratizma" [deathly affairs of bureaucracy] because he was too dead inside even for that reality.[30] Porfiry goes about the world armed with his aphorisms, ready to turn every human interaction into an empty exchange of clichés. Whenever confronted by an unexpected event that may evoke a genuine emotional reaction, he begins to form platitudes in his mind in order to remain unperturbed. He overcomes the deaths of his two sons and of his mother either by occupying himself with unfeeling requiems for the recently deceased or by rearranging their finances. As the narrator suggests, nothing from life could emotionally affect Porfiry: "He knew that *nothing* could ever catch him unawares and that nothing could ever force him to depart from that protective layer of empty and thoroughly rotten aphorisms with which he had cloaked himself head to toe. For him existed neither sorrow, nor joy, nor hatred, nor love."[31]

----

28. Todd, 102.

29. Kate Holland discusses biological degeneration in her article about the novel "The Russian Rougon-Macquart: Degeneration and Biological Determinism in *The Golovlev Family*," 15–32.

30. Saltykov-Shchedrin, 18:139.

31. Ibid., 18:118.

While in traditional Russian family novels the role of the landowner was idealized and there were expectations that a good landowner was also a benevolent family leader, in *The Golovlev Family* Saltykov-Shchedrin completely distorts the image of the landowner. Instead of commanding respect and affection from their families, Golovlev landowners are shells of the landowners that came before them. Unsurprisingly, the world that the Golovlevs govern, the gentry estate, comes to reflect their callousness and is similarly reduced to a grotesque microcosm. Whereas the estate had previously functioned like a locus of tranquility and peace, in Saltykov-Shchedrin's chronicle it emerges like a stagnant, deathly trap for the family.

III. A GROTESQUE MICROCOSM

Through Saltykov-Shchedrin's descriptions of other Golovlev family members the reader implicitly learns that at the hands of parental figures like Arina and later Porfiry, the Golovlevs are irreversibly damaged. Family members turn into vacant beings who merely live out their lives deprived of human drives. Many Golovlevs are transformed into grotesque hybrids, dehumanized through object-like or animalistic traits.

The transformation of the Golovlevs occurs in the estate where they are born and raised, the kind of space that evokes peace and tranquility in *Family Chronicle*. While Bagrovo may be a quiet corner of gentry life, Golovlevo is a distorted version of such a corner where stagnation and spiritual death underlie the facade of stable country living. Aksakov's Bagrovo is a "closed and stable world," a microcosm made up of its own routines and rituals that offer the "ideal of traditional life."[32] Saltykov-Shchedrin takes this stability and renders it so extreme that it turns into complete torpor. If Bagrovo was a removed, semimythical space of stability and ritualized action, through Golovlevo Saltykov-Shchedrin pushes stability to the extreme by recreating the estate as the most stable, closed-off space possible: the tomb.

In fact, at one point Golovlevo is described as a place of death where life, spiritual and otherwise, comes to an end. At the end of a novel, a mentally and physically defeated Anninka Golovleva, who has essentially returned to the estate to die, describes Golovlevo as a death trap. As she puts it, "Golovlevo—this was death itself [sama smert'], evil, voracious; this was death always looking for its new victim. Two uncles had died here; two cousins were dealt 'particularly severe' wounds here, the consequence of which was death; finally,

---

32. Durkin, 120.

Lyubin'ka too. . . . All deaths, all poisons, all wounds—all originated here."[33]
Anninka is not alone in making the comparison between the gentry nest and
the tomb; in fact, her statements echo Stepan's seemingly inadvertent comparison of the estate to a grave when he keeps chanting the words "Grave!
grave! grave!" while making his way back to Golovlevo.[34]

It should perhaps be expected that by living in such a tomb-like space,
many family members are immobilized and rendered incapable of action. The
Golovlevs emerge as grotesque doubles of the familiar Bagrovs, who retain
their humanity and spirituality in their quiet and mellow demeanors. By contrast the Golovlevs retain no spiritual drives and go about life as though sleep-
walking automatons.

The eldest Golovlev brother, Stepan, is struck with an inner passivity similar to Aleksei's passivity in *Family Chronicle,* but he takes this passivity too
far in that he cannot build a life for himself: he ends up living as a tramp in
the streets of Moscow. While for Aleksei Bagrov passivity had its virtues, in
Saltykov-Shchedrin's grotesque realism, it precipitates Stepan's breakdown as
a human being. "Even the last of men could do something for themselves,"
thinks Stepan to himself, "earn their living, but only he *could not do anything*
[on odin *nichego ne mozhet*]. This thought just occurred to him for the first
time."[35] Stepan's story is a testament to his inability to take action. He day-
dreams of "darovogo dovol'stva" [gratuitous allowance], an empty vision that
supplants hard work and activity.[36] No matter what he attempts—bureaucratic
service, gambling and speculation, or military service—Stepan fails miser-
ably. In Saltykov-Shchedrin's hands, Aleksei's passivity thus turns into incor-
rigible indolence. Deprived of any spiritual motivation, Stepan Golovlev is not
entirely human but rather a grotesque hybrid creature resembling objects in
its passivity and animals in being motivated by primal hunger.

His younger brother Pavel, similarly grotesque and the "perfect embodiment of someone completely lacking the will to do anything,"[37] also fails in
personal and professional spheres. The narrator mentions, "Even as a boy he
[Pavel] did not display the least inclination for studying, for games, for playing with friends: he preferred to be apart, estranged from others ['zhit' osob-
niakom, v otchuzhdenii ot liudei]."[38] Pavel is a morose version of the clownish
Stepan: just as incapable of action as his elder brother but less pleasant or

33. Saltykov-Shchedrin, 18:248.
34. Ibid., 18:29.
35. Ibid., 18:29, emphasis in the original.
36. Ibid.
37. Ibid., 18:15.
38. Ibid.

entertaining. At various points in the novel, all Pavel can do is pick his nose and drink alcohol. When given the opportunity, at his dying hour, to make a difference in the lives of his mother and nieces by leaving his estate to them, Pavel cannot act due to the inexorable listlessness that defines him. A twisted double of familiar characters like Aleksei Bagrov, Pavel is similarly grotesque and no less a hybrid creature.

The tranquil and stable reality of the family novel, as encountered in Aksakov's *Family Chronicle*, emerges in distorted form in Saltykov-Shchedrin's *The Golovlev Family*, where both the estate and its inhabitants are immersed in a grotesque torpor. If the quiet Aleksei Bagrov liked to live a calm life of contentment, this calm turns into grotesque lifelessness in the Golovlevs who have no spiritual drive and either do nothing or engage in meaningless rituals. In the end, eating is the only real activity that takes place at Golovlevo.[39]

IV. FOOD CONSUMPTION

In many respects, the single genuine act of living that punctuates the otherwise empty, rotting reality of Golovlevo is food consumption. Whereas Dostoevsky and other anti-nihilist writers used food to reveal the monstrosity of the nihilist, Saltykov-Shchedrin employs it to expose the underlying monstrosity of the gentry. Food tends to be the only interest of most Golovlevs, the only urge left in people completely devoid of spiritual energy and a means to control family members. The Golovlevs fetishize food, and virtually all their actions seem driven by the belly rather than any higher, spiritual motivations. In foregrounding food to this extent Saltykov-Shchedrin in part parodies traditional narratives of gentry life that emphasize food as a ritual that brings people together. According to Ronald LeBlanc, food was a means for writers to proclaim the importance of native values and old-fashioned customs.[40] Fictionalized meals were described in detail as a way to signify the good life in the Russian countryside, especially within the confines of the gentry estate. For instance, culinary visions flood the mind of Goncharov's Oblomov as he dreams about his native Oblomovka and attempts to recreate his childhood gastronomical paradise through Agafya, who feeds him old-fashioned food.

The earlier wholesome depiction of good as a ritual of countryside life is degraded in *The Golovlev Family*, where the importance ascribed to food signals an animalistic worldview bound up with grotesque realism. Many mem-

---

39. Todd, "Anti-Hero," 91.

40. LeBlanc, *Slavic Sins of the Flesh: Food, Sex, and Carnal Appetite in Nineteenth-Century Russian Fiction*, 16.

bers of the Golovlev family are so stripped of their higher functions that they construe food as synonymous to and the only token of a life well lived. During his journey to Golovlevo, Stepan Golovlev articulates a life philosophy that is purely gastronomic and closely intersects with the philosophy underlying the grotesque. Stepan upholds food as the only defining trait of humanity and laments that he has become dehumanized now that he is penniless and hungry. Thinking exclusively with his belly, Stepan hopes that his humanity will be restored in the rich food stores at the estate. In his fundamentally grotesque worldview, Stepan imagines that he will make peace with his mother so that "amid the rejoicing, he [could] partake of the fatted calf [upitannogo tel'tsa]."[41]

While in earlier works of literature a good appetite was viewed as a wholesome quality, in *The Golovlev Family* food consumption signifies spiritual and moral collapse. In Saltykov-Shchedrin's hands, the communal, glorious eating rites from past narratives are reduced to functions that debase individuals into grotesque, animalistic beings. Although he recreates the basic outlines of past gastronomic myths, Saltykov-Shchedrin casts a darker, Gogolian look at food consumption in *The Golovlev Family*. As LeBlanc argues, in Gogol's *Dead Souls* obsession with food suggests the "mental, moral, and emotional malnourishment," of rundown "dead souls."[42] Members of the Golovlev family similarly fixate on food for lack of any other life interest and the absence of anything resembling spirituality. Food becomes the way that parents show affection for their children. Whereas in Aksakov's chronicle food rituals allowed characters to commune with others, in *The Golovlev Family* food supplants affection, becoming an exchange currency for the parent-child relationship. Porfiry and Arina may sit around telling stories, but in reality they only exchange culinary goods with one another. Similarly, instead of helping his son Petya or saying a kind word, Porfiry sends him away with a roasted turkey. Within the grotesque microcosm that is Golovlevo, all emotional bonds are degraded to the level of physical exchange, as human beings are reduced to their bodily needs and desires.

Saltykov-Shchedrin's revision of literary myths about food, his estrangement of these earlier patterns by showing individuals who engorge themselves as morally compromised, is one of the more important features of his grotesque realism. As Bakhtin argues, "Eating and drinking are one of the most significant manifestations of the grotesque body."[43] From this perspective, in their attachment to food above all else, the Golovlevs emerge as fundamentally grotesque beings. With every family interaction reduced to the

---

41. Saltykov-Shchedrin, 18:33.
42. LeBlanc, 14.
43. Bakhtin, *Rabelais,* 281.

level of food consumption, the Golovlevs appear as grotesque hybrids, as animalistic as they are human. Having grown up in the shadow of Arina's stinginess and the deliberate way in which she begrudged everyone even a crust of bread, the Golovlevs harbor a constant and perhaps insatiable hunger for food. Due in part to this childhood privation they fixate on food, placing it at the center of their lives and renouncing their spirituality and morality for its sake. Their glorification of food reveals a process of degradation whereby everything is lowered to the level of the material, and characters live divorced from spirituality. The moment when Porfiry's sons spread butter on his communion bread provides the "perfect emblem for the book's reduction of spiritual value to basic, animal functions."[44] Like in Tolstoy's *Resurrection,* communion turns into a grotesque rite, described as "eating the body of God,"[45] so Saltykov-Shchedrin strips communion of spiritual symbolism and reduces it to mere eating.

In *The Golovlev Family,* an overwhelming emphasis on physical needs and desires leads to the defeat of personality. Characters driven exclusively by physical appetites emerge as half-animal, half-human hybrids. For instance, Stepan's entire person is reduced to mere animal functions—if he does not know where his next meal will come from, he cannot think about anything else. As the narrator puts it, Stepan "kept looking with feelings of apprehension as though he might perish from hunger at any moment like a worm [kak chervyak]."[46] At Golovlevo he sniffs around the food storage like a guard dog and gives away his part of the family inheritance for a pouch of tobacco.

The grotesque microcosm of the gentry estate stretches throughout the text, as grotesque hybridity can be encountered even among people outside the family, including the merchants whom the Golovlev girls date when they are away from the estate, most notably, the clergy. As Todd argues, "Religion is undermined by its inseparable ties to economic exploitation, gluttony, lechery, and meaningless ritual."[47] Throughout the novel, priests are often seen in connection with food and appear submissive to Porfiry, because he is the one who holds the purse strings for their churches.[48] The priest of Golovlevo, Father Alexander, seemingly also espouses a grotesque worldview and is careful not to oppose Porfiry's heretical ideas for fear that he may lose access to the Golovlevo food supply and other forms of revenue. For instance, when Porfiry's bastard child Vladimir is born, the priest does not express his disap-

---

44. Todd, "Anti-Hero," 93.
45. Tolstoy, 32:136.
46. Saltykov-Shchedrin, 18:22.
47. Todd, "Anti-Hero," 93.
48. Ibid.

proval of extramarital sex but quietly assents to Porfiry's self-serving sermons, silenced by fear of material retribution.

The Golovlevs achieve true freedom and true selfhood only when they renounce food at moments of extreme emotional duress. When they are weak, ill, or otherwise broken down and unable to enjoy the joys of the body, the Golovlevs assume human traits. After having cursed Porfiry, a dying Arina finally remembers what is most important in life and refuses to take food. Instead, her spiritual hunger is awoken as she longs for her granddaughters and implicitly also grieves for her grandson Petya, who perished over a meager three thousand rubles. Aside from starvation, suicide is another way for characters to choose the spiritual over the material. The acts of suicide in the novel—Volodya's and Lyubinka's—can be read as a way for characters to remove themselves from the world of the material. As an extreme mortification of flesh and an annihilation of the body, suicide is the ultimate rejection of the physical that allows characters to transcend the grotesquery of their worlds.

V.   GAZING INTO THE ABYSS

Saltykov-Shchedrin transforms the Russian landowner into a miserly, soulless being; eviscerates all notions of the good countryside life; and shows animalistic food consumption to be the only sign of life in the gentry. In conjunction, these elements of *The Golovlev Family* make up the novel's grotesque realism. Yet there is also an unusual, more fantastic element to the grotesque as it manifests in this work. Aside from turning familiar tropes upside down, Saltykov-Shchedrin's distortion of the family narrative in *The Golovlev Family* also distorts an essential feature of Russian realism as built by these tropes: its psychological quality. Convinced that the Russian novel was unduly focused on subjective psychological observations, Saltykov-Shchedrin used the grotesque to degrade the "dialectics of the soul" to such a degree that it became a dialectics of soullessness—a parody of the myopic, psychological focus of the family novel. Saltykov-Shchedrin's dialectics of soullessness bring forth characters who are no more than grotesque shells pulling away from reality into their empty spiritual landscapes. So empty, soulless, and grotesque are these characters that Satlykov-Shchedrin at times appears to transcend the prosaic quality of realism by leaping into the fantastic.

The Golovlevs, with their animalistic worldviews and no signs of inner spirituality, seem like complete outsiders in a literary tradition made up of psychologically complex characters like Andrei Bolkonsky or Evgeny Bazarov.

As Ilya Vinitsky argues, protagonists in *The Golovlev Family* "have become living ghosts," defined by "torpor and spiritual death."[49] The total and devastating spiritual death that defines Saltykov-Shchedrin's grotesque realism is also the basis for the fantastic elements in the novel. The unique and more extreme nature of the grotesque in *The Golovlev Family* becomes apparent when characters are left alone and the narrative veers into the fantastic. When left to their solitude, members of the Golovlev family find themselves in small, deserted rooms where their own inner emptiness grows overwhelming. These coffin-like spaces become portals into semifantastic realms as the Golovlevs lose touch with reality and immerse themselves into subjectively created limbo states, where realities grow shaky and objects lose their solidity. At such moments, these last embers of spirituality are so meager that they evoke the image of an abyss, surrounding the reader with the shadows of a fantastic world as void as the characters themselves.

Insofar as there are components of the fantastic that differ from the grotesque, it bears providing a working definition of this style, even though in *The Golovlev Family* it is essentially tied to and born of the grotesque. Unlike the grotesque, the fantastic has little in common with the day-to-day world. Whereas the grotesque shows "a disquieting estrangement of our world from itself . . . the fantastic creates a world governed by its own esoteric law."[50] It is fitting, therefore, that when the fantastic permeates and influences the grotesque, as it does in parts of *The Golovlev Family*, the grotesque can approach unexpected, possibly even supernatural, layers of existence. However, since the elements of the grotesque or fantastic in *The Golovlev Family* appear in the context of realism, the fantastic is bound up with the subjective imagination. In his discussion, Kayser distinguishes between fantastic and satirical grotesque,[51] arguing that unlike the satirical grotesque, the fantastic grotesque can be pushed to another level through phenomena like madness and dreams. Because the dreamer and the madman do not actually recreate supernatural phenomena, but merely imagine the existence of such phenomena, realist authors can use these life moments to create something larger than realism without technically breaking realist conventions or leaping into the full-blown fantastic.

The narrative moves beyond three-dimensional reality and into the sphere of the fantastic grotesque when characters are confronted with their own psychic emptiness. For instance, Stepan Golovlev is trapped alone in the small,

49. Vinitsky, *Ghostly Paradoxes: Modern Spiritualism and Russian Culture in the Age of Realism*, 113.

50. Helbling, *The Power of "Negative" Thinking: The Grotesque in the Modern World*, 16.

51. Kayser, 185.

filthy, and unlit office of the estate manager at Golovlevo, where his sense of
reality is severely constricted. Unable to go outside, look forward to the future,
or even recollect the past, Stepan is stuck in complete stasis, both physically
and spiritually. During the nighttime, he stares at the darkness, and it almost
seems as though he is walking toward a great beyond:

> His numbed imagination struggled to form any kind of images, his dead-
> ened memory endeavored to penetrate into the realm of the past, but the
> images came out shredded and senseless [razorvannye, bessmyslennye],
> while the past did not respond with a single memory. . . . Before him was
> only the present, in the form of a tightly locked prison, in which all ideas of
> space and time had vanished without a trace. The room, the stove, the three
> windows, the creaky wooden bed with its thin, worn mattress, the table with
> the bottle on it—demarcated the horizons of thought processes.[52]

The physical and mental prison Stepan inhabits, the sort of space that essentially blocks the body, numbs the mind, and turns reality into an empty abyss,
provokes hallucinatory reactions in him. With the help of alcohol, his bat-
tered and dulled mind moves past the tangible and into a strange limbo state
between life and death. The darkness of his room disappears and is replaced
by seemingly boundless space, "napolnennoe fosforicheskim bleskom" [filled
with brilliant phosphorescence].[53] Stepan is so spiritually empty inside that,
when forced to cohabitate with his own vacuity in the small confines of his
room, he completely loses his personhood. Instead of staying in the dark,
limiting, prison of objects, the intoxicated Stepan is elevated from his surroundings. In the absence of an active spiritual world, he enters a reality where
"there were no walls, no windows—nothing in fact existed but the boundless
phosphorescent void."[54]

Stepan's escape into an abyss of his own making is mirrored by similar
moments of the fantastic grotesque that result from escapes into despiritualized worlds of phantoms and hallucinatory trances by Pavel, Arina, and Porfiry. Like Stepan, the spiritually empty Pavel spends his last days trapped in his
room where he creates his own vacant fantasy world that consists of nothing
spiritual. Instead, he imagines himself and Porfiry caught in perpetual struggle against one another. As he sits in his room, completely at a distance from
reality, Pavel has no ties to other living human beings and can only trace the
"shadows [teni] wandering." In his final hours, he experiences hallucinatory

52. Saltykov-Shchedrin, 18:48.
53. Ibid.
54. Ibid.

sensations much like the ones Stepan experienced when left alone in the little office at Golovlevo.[55] It is as though Pavel's empty soul transcends all living realities, as he focuses instead on the play of light and shadow in his room. These movements create all kinds of illusions in his mind as he starts to see movement in the corner of the room, believing that his "khalat . . . dvizhetsya" [dressing gown is moving].[56]

The hallucinations are typical for all the Golovlevs, as Arina similarly experiences a flight into the fantastic as a result of her inner spiritual emptiness when alone at Pogorelka. Sitting in semidarkness, she finds that the objects in her room begin to lose their thingness. "The lamp in front of the icons," writes the narrator from Arina's point of view, "gave a deceptive appearance [obman-chivyi kharakter] to objects, so that they ceased to be objects, but seemed like outlines of objects [ochertania predmetov]."[57] Shadows, strange noises, and objects seemingly move of their own accord or turn into ghostly apparitions, thus hinting at another reality creeping underneath the visible world. Begotten by an empty, lifeless existence, these moments are glimpses into an alien realm that coexists with the reality of degradation and food consumption at Golovlevo. This empty abyss is where the Golovlevs eventually arrive after living their meaningless, grotesque lives. It is the absolute blankness at the end of a life stripped of all humanity.

Unsurprisingly, it is Porfiry, the least spiritual and perhaps most grotesque being in the novel, who is most drawn to this other layer of reality. When left sole proprietor of Golovlevo after having destroyed every single member of his family, Porfiry is more isolated than ever. Despite the acres of land at his disposal, he is trapped in his tiny study with nothing but his own emptiness. Abandoned by everyone, Porfiry withdraws into his "fantastic" sense of reality, which he populates with phantoms of his own making. He grows so detached from the real world that he wants to "Nichego by ne slyshat', nikogo by ne videt'" [see no one, hear no one], all the while expanding his fantastic reality, in which he avenges himself on the dead.[58] "He no longer felt the ground under his feet [zemlya ischezala u nego iz-pod nog] and believed he had grown wings on his back," writes the narrator, "His eyes gleamed, his lips trembled and foamed, his face turned pale and assumed a menacing look. And as his fantasies grew [po mere togo kak rosla fantaziya], the air around him became filled with phantoms with which he engaged in an imaginary

55. Ibid., 18:76.
56. Ibid., 18:77.
57. Ibid., 18:97.
58. Ibid., 18:214.

struggle [vstupal v voobrazhemuyu bor'bu]."[59] This retreat into a purely subjective world, in which Porfiry loses touch with time, space, and self, provokes a number of symptoms that can be associated with the fantastic grotesque.

Whether it is through grotesque hybridity, animalism, and automatism or the emptiness of the fantastic grotesque, Saltykov-Shchedrin completely unravels earlier narratives about the gentry family. Half-animal and half-human hybrid creatures like the Golovlevs have little in common with earlier protagonists of the Russian novel. Their spiritual worlds are emptied of deeper psychological insights; their estates have turned into tombs; and their homes have become predatory and animalistic dens of food consumption run by despotic landowners. The gentry microcosm, which had been on par with a pastoral idyll in Aksakov's *Family Chronicle*, becomes a worse Glupov than Glupov itself in *The Golovlev Family*. At least in Saltykov-Shchedrin's earlier narrative, one felt out of time and space dealing with the mad, self-destructive inhabitants of a fantastic town. In *The Golovlev Family*, the familiar setting of the estate novel makes the distortions of the grotesque sting more. This is not a random world with odd, impersonal characters. Rather, it is the family novel, the home and hearth of Russian literature turned into a grotesque microcosm. The grotesque does not pertain to a person or persons as in the early anti-nihilist novels. Instead, like at the end of *Demons*, the style is used to show an entire world stripped of spirituality and succumbing to emptiness. There is no escape from this world, and Porfiry's final, failed redemption is hardly any consolation for the terrible losses that the Russian novel has suffered in the interim between Aksakov's chronicle and Saltykov-Shchedrin's "long obituary" to the gentry family.

Though it began in the anti-nihilist genre and was later expanded by Dostoevsky and Tolstoy, grotesque realism invades the traditional literary forms of Russian realism through Saltykov-Shchedrin's *The Golovlev Family*. The novel, written in response to perceived failures in the author's contemporary novel, ultimately unravels this genre. Formerly confined to the nihilist outsider, the grotesque is redirected toward the gentry, who lose their former identities and become hybrid outsiders. By distorting Aksakov's *Family Chronicle*, one of the main sources for the portrayal of the idyllic gentry life in the Russian novel tradition, Saltykov-Shchedrin seems to "undo" past narratives. The author employs old forms to deliver new messages, showing the gentry deprived of

59. Ibid., 18:216.

spirituality and ultimately failing to adapt to the new post-Emancipation realities. After the emancipation of the serfs, even Arina Golovleva, arguably the strongest character in the novel, begins to collapse spiritually.

Nihilists, who served as a common a source for the grotesque in earlier works like *The Precipice* or *Demons,* are absent from *The Golovlev Family.* Unlike Dostoevsky, who showed nihilists as the root cause for the failure of contemporary society, Saltykov-Shchedrin refrains from all mention of nihilists, instead foregrounding the profound failure of the Russian gentry family. Without overtly invoking the agendas of the left, Saltykov-Shchedrin turns the novel form, which was beholden to the gentry, against itself. The world of the Golovlevs is rotting and caving in on itself and does not require revolutionaries to foster disorder.

This redirection of the grotesque toward the gentry, a complete turn in the novel form, also marks a new direction in Russian literature. In *Demons* and *Anna Karenina,* the grotesque already becomes a tool for exposing the failures of Russia's most powerful groups by rendering them as physically monstrous, as hybrids lacking basic humanity. This transformation, perhaps most powerfully captured in *The Golovlev Family,* ultimately becomes a prevalent trend in late Russian literature, a trend that comes into full fruition in Tolstoy's *Resurrection,* the last great Russian realist novel.

CHAPTER 5

THE GENTRY MILIEU AS GROTESQUE MICROCOSM IN TOLSTOY'S *RESURRECTION*

In thinking about the evolution of Russian grotesque realism, and particularly its expansion from a single person to what Yuri Mann calls the "grotesque microcosm,"[1] then the last Russian novel of the nineteenth century, Tolstoy's *Resurrection,* might be seen as the apotheosis of this style. As the grotesque grows more prevalent on the Russian literary scene in the late nineteenth century, it overtakes narratives of gentry life in *Demons, Anna Karenina,* and most especially *The Golovlev Family.* In this context, *Resurrection* follows as the next stage of development in Russian grotesque realism. The grotesque microcosm that comes into being in earlier works acquires broader and more defined contours in this work. As this microcosm becomes fully fleshed out, it not only supplants its earlier gentry context but overtakes the entire world of the novel.

In their experimentations with grotesque realism in the 1870s, both Dostoevsky and Saltykov-Shchedrin had Tolstoy in mind as an author of traditional gentry novels about personal happiness that sidestepped larger social questions in postreform Russia. Despite these opinions, it could be argued that Tolstoy addresses significant social issues in *Anna Karenina* in part through

---

1. Mann, *O groteske v literature,* 57.

grotesque realism. The socioeconomic and political questions are much more on the surface in *Resurrection,* where Tolstoy captures the profound discontent of the times by focusing, among many things, on underground revolutionary activity against the tsarist regime. Critics have emphasized the overtly social bent[2] of the novel, some even declaring that *Resurrection* "would not exist" without its social motifs.[3] Bakhtin, who calls *Resurrection* a "roman sotsial'no-ideologicheskii" [*socio-ideological* novel] in his 1929 preface, suggests that the novel's social motifs amount to a broad negation project. In his view, Tolstoy's primary ideological aim is to launch a "critique of all existing social relations and forms."[4]

In gestation for over ten years, the novel took a deep look at postreform Russia during one of its darkest times—when Alexander III was already reversing many of the Great Reforms and the country was in a state of profound stagnation. Critics have argued that Tolstoy captures the mood of late prerevolutionary Russia by rendering polarizing tensions "between the oppressors and the oppressed."[5] This chapter contributes to this line of argumentation by showing that grotesque realism served as an important aesthetic vehicle for depicting this social landscape in *Resurrection.* A number of scholars have already noticed that *Resurrection* does not function quite like Tolstoy's other realist novels. The presence of satire in *Resurrection* and in late Tolstoy in general has been widely recognized,[6] suggesting the possibility for the grotesque as well since the styles are related to one another. Further, both Edward Wasiolek and Harriet Murav have used the term colloquially to describe characters and images in *Resurrection* as grotesque.[7]

The familiar narratives from Tolstoy's past are at the root of the grotesque imagery in *Resurrection.* In a recent study, Justin Weir argues that in his later years "the more didactic Tolstoy repeatedly returns to his early fiction, recasting a moral light" on past narratives.[8] Working on *Resurrection* in 1891, Tolstoy expressed great enthusiasm about the prospect of writing a novel armed with his new theology. "I was so happy to . . . to start a big work of fiction

---

2. Gudzii and Maimin, "Roman L. N. Tolstogo *Voskresenie,*" 483.

3. Zhdanov, *Tvorcheskaia istoriia romana L. N. Tolstogo "Voskresenie"; materialy i nabliudeniia,* 246.

4. Bakhtin, "Preface to Volume 13: *Resurrection,*" 242–43.

5. Gudzii and Maimin, 483.

6. See, among others McLean, "Resurrection," 96–110.

7. Wasiolek mentions that the Korchagins appear grotesque to Nekhlyudov after his moral awakening, whereas Murav, who highlights the intense physicality of *Resurrection,* cites images from the prison as "grotesque." See Wasiolek, *Tolstoy's Major Fiction,* 194; Murav, "Maslova's Exorbitant Body," 37.

8. Weir, *Leo Tolstoy and the Alibi of Narrative,* 3.

[bol'shuyu khdozhestvennuyu rabotu]," he writes in his diary. "My earlier novels were an unconscious creation. . . . Now I know what is what and I can mix it all up again and work in this mix [teper' ya znayu shto shto i mogu vse smeshat' opyat' i rabotat' v etom smeshanom]."[9] He did "mix it all up again" in *Resurrection,* but his past novels were also in this mix, and he used and abused them to arrive at his new novel. Using grotesque realism to amplify his earlier device of estrangement, Tolstoy casts several concentric grotesque microcosms that lead into the other.

The prison is a grotesque microcosm distorted by injustice in which people are dehumanized, but so are the city and society at large. Many prisoners and other victims of the system, like the prostitute Maslova, emerge as grotesque hybrids. However, so do their victimizers. In Tolstoy's view virtually everyone connected to the power structure or passively observing the suffering of others is included among the victimizers, thus broadening the scope of the grotesque. Nekhlyudov and many of his gentry acquaintances, all people who could easily populate *Anna Karenina* or *War and Peace,* are depicted through the aesthetic of the grotesque and appear as soulless, shallow individuals. Their gentry microcosm as a whole is at the center of the novel's concentric grotesque circles—it serves as the site of original sin in the novel and the vantage point from which Tolstoy anatomizes the broader grotesquery plaguing the social world.

I. GROTESQUE MICROCOSMS

Before *Resurrection* came to be a novel, before even the numerous drafts leading up to its final shape, its plot had been a true story, with a social scope that extended beyond the gentry realities of Tolstoy's earlier novels. A. F. Koni, who served as prosecutor for the St. Petersburg court district, recounted the story that would blossom into a full-blown novel by Tolstoy in June 1887. Koni told Tolstoy about a nobleman who visited his chambers, asking permission to correspond with a female prisoner named Rozaliya Oni. A prostitute from a brothel of the sordid type in the Haymarket, Rozaliya was sentenced to four months in prison after stealing one hundred rubles from an intoxicated "guest." The nobleman informed Koni of his intentions to marry the woman, asking him to intervene at the jail to make the wedding possible. Koni did his best to dissuade him, but his efforts failed, as Rozaliya happily assented to the marriage proposal. The two shared several visits at the jail, and the wedding

---

9. Tolstoy, *Polnoe sobranie sochinenii,* 52:5–6. All translations are my own.

would likely have taken place had Rozaliya not unexpectedly died of typhoid. Distraught over the loss, the nobleman took the money he had set aside as dowry for his fiancée and donated it to the prison for the benefit of female prisoners and children.[10]

A few months later, Koni would discover the reasons behind the man's shocking actions. As he learned, Rozaliya had been the daughter of a Finnish widower who did handiwork for a wealthy woman in St. Petersburg. The widower developed liver cancer and begged the woman to take care of his daughter, who would soon become orphaned. Honoring his request, the wealthy woman took Rozaliya into her home where she lived for seventeen years. However, her time at the noblewoman's home came to an abrupt end when a young student related to the lady of the house seduced Rozaliya. She became pregnant with his child, was thrown out by the wealthy woman, gave the baby up to an orphanage, and eventually ended up as a prostitute in the Haymarket. The student was the same man who proposed marriage years later.[11]

Tolstoy was obviously taken by this unusual story, which was at the core of his last novel. As Lidiya Gromova-Opulskaia shows, when the author began the transformation of the Koni story into a novel, he struggled with the order of the contents, simultaneously drawn to the man's gentry background and Rozaliya's subsequent downward spiral. Initially, Tolstoy began the novel with the seduction at a locus that was obviously familiar to him, the gentry estate. However, after completing the first full draft of the novel 1895, he felt that the narrative had been "lozhno nachato" [falsely begun] and that he "dolzhno nachat' s nee [Maslova]" [must start with her].[12] In the end Tolstoy did indeed "start with her," beginning not with the idyllic gentry estate, but on a substantially darker note with depictions of the prison squalor where Maslova lands after her seduction.

As a result of this chronological reversal, we see Tolstoy move out of the gentry microcosm that had been a staple in his earlier novels. The novel commences more broadly with Tolstoy's celebrated device of "defamiliarization" or *ostranenie*, which launches the reader into an alien, unnatural reality. In an image of an urban spring with its fragile beauty, people are making every effort to suppress nature:

No matter how hard men tried, one hundred thousand of them gathering in one small place, no matter how they disfigured that land where they had crowded themselves, no matter how they paved the land with stones so that

10. Zhdanov, 4–5.
11. Ibid.
12. Opul'skaia, "Psikhologicheskii analiz v romane 'Voskresenie,'" 320–21.

nothing could grow in it, no matter how they cleared away every blade of grass, no matter how they filled the air with coal and gas, no matter how they cut down every tree and chased away every animal and bird—spring was spring, even in the city [vesna byla vesnoyu dazhe i v gorode].[13]

According to Victor Shklovsky, Tolstoy's use of defamiliarization often consists of the author's refusal to "call a thing by its name," instead "describ[ing] it as if it were perceived for the first time."[14] In his depiction of spring in the city, Tolstoy conveys an original view on Russian urbanization, and perhaps all urbanization, by taking the stance of someone unfamiliar with how cities come about and refusing to acknowledge urbanization as an established historical fact. The city as a locus is not properly identified until the very end of the sentence.

Moving from the device to its effects, one can note that the city is shown as an unnatural place that disrupts natural splendor and the flow of seasons. The device of defamiliarization projects a wide net in the narrative—the city as a whole is rendered as an unnatural contraption, thus prefiguring Tolstoy's treatment of every institutional layer of Russian society in *Resurrection*. As Mikhail Bakhtin argues, "This wide and purely philosophical picture of the urban spring, the struggle between the good spring and the evil city culture . . . sets the tone of all subsequent exposures of human inventions: prisons, courts, high society, and others."[15] In the opening sentence, the juxtaposition of nature to the aberrations of social reality—a reality that depletes the earth of its fecundity and drives away animals—suggests that as upon transitioning from the large-scale urban panorama into the city's various institutional divisions, the reader will simply alternate between concentric layers of the same world built upon unnatural and often immoral premises. As the narrative gaze gravitates toward more concrete layers of this world, the grotesque helps the author sketch out these unnatural and dehumanizing spaces.

In many respects, the image of the city as an aberration of nature might be said to constitute the widest layer of grotesque realism in *Resurrection,* or the widest concentric circle. From this broader estrangement of how the world is supposed to be, the text moves to the prison, which exemplifies institutionalized unnaturalness and dehumanization. As the reader learns, "In the [prison] corridor the air was heavy with the germs of typhoid and the smell of sewage, tar and putrefaction."[16] The stench of excrement and disease demonstrate

---

13. Tolstoy, 32:3.
14. Shklovsky, *Theory of Prose,* 6.
15. Bakhtin, "Preface to Volume 13," 245.
16. Tolstoy, 32:4.

the cruelty and inhumanity that define the prison. These phenomena can be associated with the barren land presented in the novel's opening and seem to follow through the pattern whereby morally unjust social institutions are depicted as an aberration of natural principles. Prisoners appear disturbed and are stripped of spirituality: some crouch in the corner; some are wild and mad; some crass, some violent, and all dehumanized by the terrible prison setting.

The grotesque centers on the bodies of the dehumanized prisoners. Although Maslova's grotesquery revolves around her sexual defilement, one can also see how the prison degrades her to the level of a grotesque object. The narrator observes that Maslova "was pale with the pallor peculiar to people who have been shut in for a long time" and that her appearance resembles that of "potatoes kept in a cellar," which sprout shoots.[17] The comparison between Maslova and the potato implies her dehumanization and deformation in the prison's unnatural conditions. The prison, just like the estate in *The Golovlev Family*, could be seen as another grotesque microcosm that turns people into distorted, grotesque versions of themselves.

Indeed, toward the end of the novel one can clearly observe the broader damage that the prison and society at large, two grotesque microcosms with blurring boundaries, cause for the individuals at their mercy. When the prisoners are headed on their long march to Siberia, their dehumanization and reduction to the level of half-human and half-object hybrids is captured in full detail. Dressed alike, walking in line, the prisoners look like a giant machine making its way through the city. Tolstoy describes this procession in detail, highlighting its dehumanizing nature:

> The procession was so long that the men in the front were out of sight by the time luggage carts and feeble-bodied prisoners were on the move. . . . It had become very hot. There was no wind, and the dust raised by thousands of feet constantly stood over the prisoners, as they moved to the center of the road. They were walking with a quick step, and the slow-trotting horse of Nekhlyudov's cab could barely catch up to them. Row after row walked unknown, strange and fearful creatures dressed alike, thousands of feet shod alike, all in step, swinging their arms as if to keep up spirits. There were so many of them, they all looked so alike and their circumstances were so extraordinarily odd, that to Nekhlyudov they no longer seemed like men, but peculiar and dreadful creatures of some sort [osobennye, strashnye sushchestva].[18]

17. Ibid., 32:21.
18. Ibid., 32:330.

The description of the march of prisoners, by way of Nekhlyudov's gaze, as "strange fearful creatures" or as "peculiar and dreadful creatures of some sort," indicates that due to their social status, these men and women are no longer viewed as human subjects. They have morphed—at least in the eyes of society—into something strange and unnatural, a grotesque, multi-headed body.

The image of prisoners set into motion by an overwhelming social force has strong grotesque overtones. Marching forward in automatized fashion, the prisoners give the impression that they are blindly following orders and have become empty vessels for societal mandates. Prisoners are driven by an impersonal, societal force, turned into automatons of the system. These individuals are robbed of personal identities, made to wear uniforms, had half of their heads shaven, and have been sent on a journey that, for many of them, will end in death. The implication that the prisoners are nothing more than grotesque automatons of the system is echoed throughout the novel, perhaps most saliently in the words of the female revolutionary Nekhlyudov meets during his visit to St. Petersburg. "I realized that I was no longer a human being, but had become a *thing* [veshch'],"[19] she says when discussing her first arrest.

II. THE GENTRY ESTATE TURNED GROTESQUE MICROCOSM

If the prison is a demarcated, grotesque microcosm symptomatic of the injustice of society at large, the blame for the evils of this society falls on the most powerful and most privileged. In this case, the responsibility falls on the gentry microcosm, which emerges as warped and distorted in *Resurrection*. Tolstoy, who had so struggled with the novel's beginning, onlyintroduces the reader to the gentry estate indirectly, in the course of telling Maslova's story. In this initial introduction, the gentry world is estranged from how it was normally conceived and rendered as a dehumanizing space where people are degraded and treated no better than livestock. As the narrative moves into Maslova's life story, the familiar world of the author's earlier writings is retrospectively deconstructed through a vein of unnaturalness. The sixth child of the daughter of a serf woman, Maslova had no inherent value as a human being. In an affront to nature, she was nearly destined to die from birth and survives only when the lady of the house, Nekhlyudov's aunt, accidentally enters the cowshed where Maslova's mother is nursing. In the vicious tone of an enraged observer of horrible facts, Tolstoy tells of how Maslova's mother

---

19. Ibid., 32:294.

was treated no better than a farm animal, which her children, like the many peasant children Nekhlyudov sees when he visits his country estates, are deemed expendable. The narrator tells of Maslova's strange upbringing and her partial and temporary redemption: she grew up feeling like half a servant, half a young lady, because Nekhlyudov's aunts differed in how they treated her. Maslova's temporary humanization quickly vanishes, as she is cast out of the gentry microcosm when Nekhlyudov seduces and impregnates her. At this point, Maslova, like her mother before her, is treated like livestock, as her baby dies from illness and neglect, meeting the same fate its mother should have met as an infant. After various incidents of sexual harassment and being treated like an object for the gratification of male sexual desire, Maslova embraces her objectification and winds up a prostitute.

The gentry estate had been an essential space of the Tolstoyan novel, virtually created for the replication of generations and brimming with organic energies. In *Anna Karenina,* at Levin's Pokrovskoe estate, humans and animals alike reproduce successfully: the Levins conceive a child and Pava the cow gives birth to a calf. Yet in Maslova's life story, the familiar space of gentry estate is almost unrecognizable and redefined as a site of death and sterility where people are not nurtured, but rather degraded and dehumanized to the level of grotesque objects. While innocent babies die in the barn from neglect and squalor, spinster aunts with no heirs except for Nekhlyudov live upstairs. Such a space is no bucolic haven. The natural progression of generations that occurs in other Tolstoyan novels is obstructed in *Resurrection.* If the world in *War and Peace* and *Anna Karenina* was full of health and virility, in *Resurrection* that world appears diseased and decayed, no cleaner than the prison with its rancid air and contagious typhoid. The most disturbing sign of the grotesque degradation of the individual in this formerly bucolic space is the fact that virtually all children, including Maslova's siblings who died in infancy, her own child, and the peasant children whom Nekhlyudov encounters during his visit to his estates, either do not live past infancy or seem at risk for illness or death.[20] The wizened, strange-looking peasant baby that Nekhlyudov encounters during his countryside exploration midway through the novel embodies the grotesquery of the gentry nest. Half-old man and half-child, the baby is a hybrid, grotesque offspring of an unnatural world.

The only deviation from the rendition of the gentry world as grotesque can be found in Nekhlyudov's flashbacks about his acquaintance with Maslova,

20. Murav takes note of the plight of infants in the novel and argues that *Resurrection* is a "motherless utopia" where Tolstoy replaces the birth model with the "resurrection" of ancestors advocated by Nikolai Fedorov. One exception is the governor's daughter, whom he insists Nekhlyudov meet in Siberia. See Murav, 41–42.

which mark a brief return of an earlier Tolstoyan narrative voice. Nekhlyudov retreats to the country because "it was quiet" and "there were no distractions."[21] Tolstoy shows Nekhlyudov to be in perfect "obshchenie s prirodoi" [communion with nature][22] as he wanders the fields or stops for a nap somewhere in the garden. It is that his romance with Maslova commences in this idyllic, quasi-pastoral haven as the "innocent" love "between an innocent young man and a similarly innocent young girl."[23] The natural world punctuates every moment of these early encounters between the characters as they accidentally kiss and Maslova wipes her face on a white lilac from a nearby bush. These short-lived moments of narrative beauty are charged with purity; this is Tolstoy the realist at his finest.

These chapters in *Resurrection* have been lauded by critics as reminiscent of narrative descriptions in *War and Peace* and *Anna Karenina,* and as the best, most artistic portions of the book. The reminiscences tell a story not so different from the one recounted during Maslova's narrative, but we can note a clear stylistic clash between the curt, almost telegraphic sentences in Maslova's story and Nekhlyudov's more elaborate and literary flashbacks. As an indication perhaps of his unwillingness to get caught up in the narratives of his past, Tolstoy presents this positive depiction of the countryside only after presenting an image of the gentry estate as a space of grotesque degradation. Maslova's story preemptively desecrates the benevolence and innocence conjured in the reminiscences. Since the plot moves from innocence to seduction, to prostitution, this same countryside also becomes the site of original sin—the spiritual innocence of the reminiscences is degraded to the level of grotesque sexual corruption and prostitution.

Grotesque narratives from the novel's present constantly encroach upon these beautiful, nearly pastoral renditions of the past. The reader's and Nekhlyudov's nostalgia-ridden aesthetic enjoyments are fragmented, as flashbacks of the gentry estate alternate with the anatomical descriptions of the corpse of the merchant Maslova is accused of killing. Nekhlyudov remembers his past with Maslova while confronted with the nauseatingly detailed autopsy report of the merchant's various bodily organs. He mentally conflates this body with his past treatment of Maslova at his aunt's estate. "Katyusha's life," thinks Nekhlyudov, "and the pus that seeped out of the [merchant's] nostrils, and the eyes coming out of their sockets, and his act with her, all were, it seemed to him, objects that belonged to one and the same category and he was sur-

---

21. Tolstoy, 32:43.
22. Ibid., 32:47.
23. Ibid., 32:45.

rounded from all sides and swallowed by these objects."[24] Nekhlyudov's seduction of Maslova within the bounds of the gentry microcosm is thus equated to
the grotesque, dehumanized corpse of the merchant. Indirectly, one is induced
to condemn and mistrust the enchanting yet ultimately misleading beauty of
the past, for it leads Malsova to prostitution and indirectly begets the grotesque monster that is the merchant.

III. THE OBJECTIFIED SUBJECT

The corpse of the merchant that spills out from every orifice, breaching
boundaries between the inside and the outside, functions as a focal point for
the grotesque in *Resurrection*. An assortment of pus, enlarged organs, and
rotting skin, the merchant's corpse almost cannot add up to a whole human
being. This grotesque body that reaches outwardly and seemingly "poison[s]
the air of the whole novel"[25] is depicted piecemeal like a medical artifact.
Indeed, the merchant is objectified to the point that he is not even given a
proper human name. As in previous works like Leskov's *Cathedral Folk,* where
the corpse is the quintessential grotesque body, a hybrid between the human
and the object, so also does the merchant's body assume an important role in
how Tolstoy structures his grotesque realism. The exhaustive descriptions of
this nameless, grotesque body, this *it,* are not accidental, nor do they function
like extraneous realistic details. The evocation of the gentry estate alongside
the image of the merchant has a damning influence on the reader's perception
of that cultural space.

Tolstoy assigns additional representational roles to the body of the merchant. By way of this individual who is dehumanized and reduced to a pound
of flesh, the author anatomizes the societal malaises of despiritualization and
dehumanization. In its corpulence and ugliness, the corpse of the merchant
throws a grotesque light on the world of the novel at large. The corpse serves
as a metonymic reflection of the wider loss of spiritual identity in the novel—
a loss also signaled by the transformation of Katyusha into the prostitute
Lyubka and the degradation of her spiritual romance with Nekhlyudov to the
level of sexual gratification.

Through Nekhlyudov's mental conflation of his past with Maslova to the
merchant's body, Tolstoy also hints at her fall as a character as marked by
the depletion of her spirituality. He forges a connection between the dead

---

24. Ibid., 32:69.
25. Bayley, *Tolstoy and the Novel,* 258.

body and the sexualized body of the prostitute, which fits with his views on sex as spiritually destructive. As we have seen, these views are already partly reflected in *Anna Karenina,* where a link is forged between the dying body of Nikolai and the adulteress's sexualized body, as desire also strips Anna of her spiritual essence. In *Resurrection,* where the pregnant Maslova contemplates but does not carry out suicide, Tolstoy equates her sexually degraded body to a corpse.

The degree to which Maslova is "dead" while still alive is best illustrated by comparing her to past Russian heroines. Going as far back as Karamzin's "Poor Liza," suicide provides tidy closure in many Russian stories of amorous affairs gone astray. Aside from the example of Anna Karenina, Turgenev's "A Quiet Spot"—which is mentioned as Maslova's favorite work—also ends with the suicide of the heroine. In light of such literary precedents, the moment in *Resurrection* when Maslova also considers suicide as an escape becomes especially poignant. "A train will come," she thinks to herself. "I'll throw myself under and all will be over."[26] Eventually, however, Nekhlyudov's baby moves inside her and Maslova gives up the idea. Yet at this same moment she renounces God, embraces drinking and smoking, and enters the path that ends in prostitution. Although Maslova does not end up under a train like Anna Karenina, her repeated sexual violations have buried her soul so deep into the subconscious that she may well be dead—a thing-like, grotesque body not so different from the oozing object that is the merchant's corpse.

Tolstoy shows Maslova in a state of living death as a prostitute, utterly devoid of spirituality and burying herself in alcohol and cigarettes. Maslova goes from being a reader of Russian literature and a spiritually pure soul to an intoxicated, sexualized body. "This woman is dead" [mertvaya zhenshchina], thinks Nekhlyudov to himself when he first sees her at the jail.[27] As Tolstoy implies, Maslova's degradation begins when she is reduced to merely her body during the initial consummation of her affair with Nekhlyudov in the gentry estate. Throughout the seduction scene we witness the "materialization" of Maslova as Nekhlyudov degrades her, approaching her as a body rather than as an integrated person with an inner spiritual world. Nekhlyudov hears Maslova's words, which express resistance and beseech him to stop the sexual act, but he gives preference to her body language. He hears her say, "'How can you? Your aunts will hear,'" but feels that her "whole being cried, 'I am yours.'"[28] As Tolstoy notes, "it [is] only *this* [body language] that Nekhlyudov underst[ands]." While Maslova rejects his advances in words, Nekhlyudov

---

26. Tolstoy, 32:131.
27. Ibid., 32:149.
28. Ibid., 32:62.

believes that her body welcomes them.[29] Everything in Maslova is lowered to this bodily level.

This initial perception of Maslova as nothing more than a body precipitates her downward spiral toward prostitution, at which point she participates in and abets her own degradation. In fact, Maslova agrees to get her yellow card, which sanctions her practice of prostitution, because, as Tolstoy mentions, she "imagined herself in bright yellow silk trimmed with black velvet—décolleté—and she could not resist so she handed over her identity papers."[30] The image that Maslova constructs of herself is an exclusively physical one. In this moment, she no longer views herself as a multidimensional person who might be spiritually hurt by prostitution. Rather, she constructs an exclusively physical image of herself by admiring her own physical attractiveness and lavish dress. Like Anna Karenina, who essentially morphs into her own portrait, or the Golovlev women, Anninka and Lyubinka, who are damaged at the gentry estate in their youth, so Maslova seems spiritually broken and renounces her identity for the sake of this attractive frozen frame and a life of physical objectification.

Yet physical degradation and the loss of spiritual identity are not limited to the body of the prostitute but emerge as systemic phenomena. In the most basic terms, if Maslova is spiritually dead and must be awoken in the course of the novel, then her seducer, Nekhlyudov, is no less spiritually suffocated in his life. After we see Maslova's degradation, Tolstoy turns the narrative to a depiction of Nekhlyudov. Although he may not be as monstrous as Dostoevsky's Pyotr Verkhovensky or Leskov's Termosesov, with his thin hair, stout neck, and decayed teeth, Nekhlyudov is quite unappealing. Tolstoy introduces Nekhlyudov in a manner similar to Stiva Oblonsky in the earlier *Anna Karenina,* but Tolstoy is more forgiving of the latter's indiscretions. In contrast, he indicts Nekhlyudov for his romantic appetites. At the beginning of the novel, Nekhlyudov is the same crass creature that ruins Maslova. Not overtly grotesque, he eschews spirituality while being exclusively preoccupied with his pampered body and his romantic entanglements.

IV. THE GROTESQUE WORLD

From the merchant's corpse, to Maslova's "exorbitant body,"[31] to the detailed physical descriptions of the prisoners, to Nekhlyudov's corporeality, *Resur-*

---

29. Ibid.
30. Ibid., 32:10.
31. Murav, 35.

rection stands out as a novel where individuals are depicted and treated first and foremost as bodies. There are a number of microcosms in which individuals are reduced to the level of grotesque hybrids, and these feed into one another. Outside the prison, not only is the novel's purported gentry protagonist, Nekhlyudov, degraded, but his entire gentry circle in Moscow is similarly depicted as grotesque. Respected members of the gentry, like Nekhlyudov's acquaintances, the Korchagins, are shown as devoid of spirituality and reduced to grotesque bodies. The Korchagins belong to the same circles as the Rostovs from *War and Peace* or the Shcherbatskys from *Anna Karenina* and take part in some of the same social activities, but they are emptied of their essence and stand as grotesque doubles to these earlier characters. The amoral Countess Lydia and Princess Betsy from *Anna Karenina* or the perverse Kuragins from *War and Peace,* who were the anomaly in the earlier works, might be viewed as their literary predecessors in Tolstoy.

When visiting the Korchagins for dinner the evening following Maslova's trial, Nekhlyudov is confronted with an alien and grotesque side of them. Tolstoy directly hints at the unusual nature of Nekhlyudov's perception during this dinner. "At that moment," writes Tolstoy about Nekhlyudov, "strange images [strannye obrazy] rose in his imagination for some unaccountable reason."[32] These strange images take the shape of various body parts that are singled out and force their way into Nekhlyudov's field of vision. The false teeth and lidless eyes of old Korchagin, his red face and smacking lips, stick out to Nekhlyudov. Instead of visualizing a man, Nekhlyudov sees body parts extracted from the whole of Korchagin. In Tolstoy's description, old Korchagin is a collection of unappealing appendages menacingly protruding outward. These images and many others in the scene recall Bakhtin's arguments about the grotesque as a style of unwieldy body parts that disrupt smooth, shapely imagery.

Aside from the appalling Korchagin, his wife, daughter, and their guests are similarly repulsive to the eye. Missy, whom Nekhlyudov considers marrying, has wrinkles on her aging face, sharp elbows, and angular fluffed hair. Her even more decrepit, paralyzed mother, trying to look younger than her age, is so physically unappealing that she is rightfully terrified of being seen in the light of the sun or without her expensive silk outerwear. Looking at her as if for the first time, Nekhlyudov is disgusted and appalled to the point that he has to stop imagining what her shoulders look like under the multiple layers of expensive fabric. "He [Nekhlyudov] imagined them [Sophia Vasilevna's shoulders] in their natural state," writes Tolstoy, "but this image

---

32. Tolstoy, 32:97.

was too hideous; he tried to banish it from his mind."[33] Nekhlyudov also sees another guest, Kolossov, whom he also imagines without the protective, form-giving layers of clothing, only as "a stomach like a melon, a balding skinny, and whip-like arms."[34] Like Sophia Vasilevna's shoulders, the protruding belly assumes grotesque qualities.

The Korchagins are grotesque not only in their physical appearance but also in their behavior. When they converse about various cultural events, Nekhlyudov cannot help noticing that they do so simply out of habit, without personal investment. "Nekhlyudov saw," writes Tolstoy about a conversation between Korchagina and Kolossov, "that neither of them cared about the play or about one another other, and that if they talked, it was only to satisfy the physical necessity to exercise the muscles of the throat and tongue after eating."[35]

The ugliness of gentry world becomes apparent in Tolstoy's depiction of Filip, Sophia Vasilevna's footman. Filip is the only one in the Korchagin household not described as a grotesque being. Tolstoy describes him as "muscular, broad-chested, and handsome," with "strong legs and well-developed calves." The footman is so handsome that he is even equated with a "naturshchikom" [an artist's model] in Nekhlyudov's mind.[36] In this sense, the socially inferior Filip serves as a point of reference for the reader, an example of natural beauty and strength in contrast to the gentry microcosm embodied by the Korchagins and their friends. If there ever was a classical ideal, Filip is that person, yet the world he inhabits is so unnatural and paradoxical that he must follow every whim of the paralyzed, frail Korchagina. "The strong, handsome Filip at once concealed his impatience, and went on doing what the feeble, ema-ciated, artificial creature commanded of him," writes Tolstoy as Filip closes the curtains in response to Korchagina's commands.[37] The emphasis here is on the unnatural foundations of a world in which a weaker, paralyzed, and unattractive being like Korchagina can to give orders to Filip, who is naturally superior to her. It is this unnaturalness that delineates the larger grotesque-ness of the scene.

The loss of identity at both high and low levels of society is symptomatic of socially endorsed processes of dehumanization that are directed toward those at the mercy of society but that can unexpectedly reflect back on the privileged. If prisoners have been reduced to grotesque automatons by those

---

33. Ibid., 32:99.
34. Ibid., 32:97.
35. Ibid., 32:95.
36. Ibid., 32:99.
37. Ibid.

in power, the institutionalized dehumanization evident in the prison is not an isolated, peripheral phenomenon. The prison is the center of the alien, estranged world of *Resurrection*. It has a spider-like reach that stretches from one concentric layer to the next. Directly or indirectly, virtually everyone on the outside participates in or validates the abominations of the prison. Tolstoy maps out these connections through the various spheres in the novel. The prison makes captives out of everyone it touches—characters like jailers, lawyers, judges—and those with official roles in the prison superstructure are as much prisoners of it as are Maslova and Simonson. Nekhlyudov also has ties to the prison, both because of the initial seduction but also because he participates in Maslova's unjust sentencing. Everyone who is a member of the jury at Maslova's trial is connected to the prison, as is everyone who has ever had to serve as juror. By its very nature, a participatory legal system certifies that this last group is large and indiscriminate. Family links implicate even more people: Mariette, like Nekhlyudov's aunt, is joined to the system by way of her husband. Individuals who have no connections to the prison, but who permit such injustices to continue by virtue of their indifference, like the Korchagins, are also indirectly tied to the institution. An individual like Missy's father, old Korchagin, who was gratuitously cruel during his tenure in the military, is doubly connected to the prison, because his own inherent cruelty fits with the general mentality that inspires the institution.

The subtle signs of the decline of the gentry in *Anna Karenina* turn into a complete tour de force in *Resurrection*. As Tolstoy shows, the rich and mighty like the Korchagins and others have themselves lost their basic humanity and wander about like grotesque soulless bodies driven by impersonal forces. Irrespective of whether they have ever set foot in a prison, all these people are shown to be guilty of misdeeds toward their fellow men. They dehumanize others, degrading them to the level of grotesque hybrids, while becoming dehumanized themselves. "There is a thing called government service," writes Tolstoy, "which allows men to treat other men like they were things [veshchi]."[38] He elaborates on this notion at various points in the book by suggesting that in dealing with prisoners, those in power act as though prisoners were not fellow human beings but inanimate objects.

Tolstoy extends this argument about the dehumanization of others also to the law, which is revealed to be a tremendous impersonal force that supplants the individual's free will. Those involved in legal processes do not think about the special circumstances of each individual case but instead blindly apply legal principles. Even Nekhlyudov's friend Selenin, who had a personal

---

38. Ibid., 32:352.

sense of right and wrong in his youth, has relinquished individual morality for the principles of the law, applying these principles to every circum-
stance while allowing his own opinions and actions to be exclusively guided
by them. Indeed, countless individuals in the novel renounce their personalities and personal morality by deferring to impersonal forces like the law. Some
even subjugate their personal opinions to more ridiculous and more arbitrary
forces. For instance, the third juror in the opening of the novel counts steps
and mechanically decides life questions based on the results of these count-
ing processes.

As a reflection of a larger grotesquery and failure of morality in Russian
society, the most grotesque, automated, and soulless being in the novel is
Toporov, Chief Procurator of the Most Holy Synod. Like in *Demons*, where
holy or venerated men are as soulless as everyone else, or like in *The Golovlev Family*, where the priest succumbs to Yudushka's grotesque worldview,
so Toporov, spiritual guardian of society in *Resurrection*, is fundamentally
grotesque. As Hugh McLean points out, this character is "an obvious caricature" of the archconservative Chief Prosecutor Konstantin Pobedonostsev,
who was a major advisor to Alexander III.[39] During a visit to Toporov in order
to appeal the case of the sectarians, Nekhlyudov notes that this man "in the
depths of his soul . . . really believed in nothing."[40] An underlying nihilism is
obvious in the "pale, immobile mask [nepodvizhnaya maska]" plastered on
his face.[41] Like Stavrogin, Toporov embodies the spiritual ossification of the
Russian citizen after the Great Reforms. He is no more than a hybrid between
man and automaton. In fact, when he shockingly decides to intercede for the
sectarians by personally settling the affair, Nekhlyudov describes Toporov as
a grotesque body at work, moving about automatically to accomplish a task
in which he has no emotional investment. "Nekhlyudov continued to stand,"
writes Tolstoy, "looking down on the narrow bald skull, at the hand with thick
blue veins swiftly moving the pen, and wondered why this man, who was
obviously indifferent to everything, was doing what he was doing, and why he
has doing it with such care. What for?"[42] Nekhlyudov cannot discern the reason why this grotesque body with its narrow bald skull is moving so swiftly,
but it is evident that it is not out of personal morality but rather the impetus
to save face for his institution driving him to action.

39. McLean, 107.
40. Tolstoy, 32:297.
41. Ibid., 32:298.
42. Ibid., 32:299.

V. SPIRITUAL AWAKENING AND THE REDEMPTION OF THE GROTESQUE

The portrayal of one of the main guardians of spirituality in Russian society as a soulless automaton fits with Tolstoy's broader picture of Russian reality as a world in which spiritually is in steep decline. In a scene that has become notorious for precipitating the author's 1901 excommunication by the Holy Synod, Tolstoy also degrades the Eucharist as a fundamentally grotesque ritual stripped of all spirituality. The children in the prison take communion as the priest wipes their mouths and "sing[s] a song about the children eating God's flesh and drinking His blood."[43] Scholars have understood these descriptions as highly satirical,[44] but the effect they produce is also grotesque. Not only are characters degraded and reduced to mere bodies, but also the mystery of their deity is degraded into flesh and blood. The moment compares to the placement of butter on the communion bread in *The Golovlev Family,* another pivotal moment in grotesque realism when faith is degraded.

Despite the clear desecration Tolstoy associates with canonical orthodoxy, he puts on display other sources of faith in the novel that, unlike in other works addressed so far, allow for the redemption of the grotesque. One non-religious source of faith that emerges in the novel is the ideology of the revolutionaries, which shapes how Tolstoy views this group. Unlike the official keeper of the faith, Toporov, the revolutionaries have powerful, deep-seated beliefs that shape their morality and facilitate altruism and caring about their fellow man.

One of the most obvious manifestations of the faith of the revolutionaries is reflected in the fact that these characters seem immune to Tolstoy's poetics of the grotesque. In an interesting reversal of the anti-nihilist novel, left-wing political prisoners and successors of the earlier nihilists are some of the only spiritual characters in *Resurrection.* If in *The Precipice, Cathedral Folk,* and even *Demons,* the social outsiders are the materialistic monsters who pollute society with their unfeeling ways, in *Resurrection* the revolutionaries are the only characters still capable of spirituality. In his depiction of the revolutionaries Tolstoy eschews the grotesque and dwells on their spirituality as reflected in their eyes. Instead of seeing locked-up bodies, we see Maria Pavlova's beautiful and soulful eyes, or large sad eyes looking through peepholes in solitary prison cells. The eye, as Bakhtin points out, is not very relevant to the grotesque, unless it is somehow deformed.[45]

---

43. Ibid., 32:136.
44. McLean, 101.
45. Bakhtin, *Rabelais,* 316.

Although Tolstoy does not agree with the ideas of the revolutionaries, which he occasionally also derides, he is drawn to their passion. Unlike the hollow gentry, the revolutionaries are fired up by deep, nearly religious faith in their cause. This morality is contingent upon their faith in their cause, which allows revolutionaries to rise above the grotesque degradation and lasciviousness that dominate the gentry and societal circles. Like Tolstoy himself, Simonson and Maria Pavlova, although members of the gentry, reject sexuality and instead privilege helping others. While traveling to Siberia, Simonson and Pavlova give up their seats in the prisoner cart to others who are more in need of accommodations. A far cry from the Korchagins, both fall outside the corrupt gentry microcosm and seem to embody the soul of the Russian gentry in *Resurrection*.

Maslova's friendship with Simonson and Pavlova facilitates her spiritual "resurrection," giving the reader a perspective on these soulful revolutionaries. By getting to know individuals like Pavlova or Simonson, embracing their emphasis on spirituality, and helping others, Maslova is also restored to her more spiritual and altruistic self. She abjures her earlier life of prostitution and chooses to go to Siberia with Simonson, whose sexless love she prefers to the earlier attachment to Nekhlyudov, which still contains elements of conventional romantic attachment, the very thing that the late Tolstoy disavowed.

If the abstract, ideological faith of the revolutionaries becomes Maslova's redemption, Nekhlyudov has a properly Tolstoyan spiritual awakening. By the novel's end, he reads the Gospels as if for the first time and absorbs the meaning of the verses in an unexpected, life-changing manner. His great epiphany is that individuals should live remembering God by focusing on love for others and spirituality. This religious epiphany completes Nekhlyudov's "resurrection" in the novel. He transforms from the self-satisfied, amoral person interested only in the life of the body as reflected in senseless affairs into a spiritual person who aims to transcend physicality for the spirit.

Resurrection ends with what looks like the beginning of Nekhlyudov's life journey as governed by his new moral code. In the context of the phenomenon of the grotesque, this journey, as well as Maslova's spiritual awakening, marks the first case of a religious or spiritual redemption within the bounds of grotesque realism. Many grotesque characters we have seen so far, including Yudas Golovlev and others, seem permanently bound to their own grotesquery, as their souls appear atrophied to the point of nonexistence. The instances of spiritual renewal in *Resurrection*, however, suggest that individuals entangled in sexual desire and spiritual debasement can liberate themselves from their state. As Tolstoy insists, no matter what the degradation, one's soul can always be brought back to life.

In the three decades since the grotesque in the Russian realist novel began, one can note a complete turnaround in the political affiliation of the grotesque as the gentry insiders and society at large turn grotesque, while the leftist revolutionaries are the only moral figures. What this reversal within grotesque realism suggests is that the gentry world, which had up until then been the heart of the novel, is no longer a suitable space for narration. Tolstoy negates this space through his aesthetic of the grotesque. The few positive or neutral glimpses of the gentry estate in the novel are situated in the past, whereas Nekhlyudov's depictions from his countryside travels capture a terrifying reality where children and adults perish alongside one another. There is no beauty or goodness left in the gentry microcosm—at the end of the novel, after pages and pages spent in the confines of the prison or en route to Siberia, the narrative seems as rootless and homeless as its protagonist.

While gentry spaces in the novel seem irredeemable, Nekhlyudov and Maslova are redeemed. Maslova is given a difficult path in which to live out her new convictions. Yet Tolstoy does not explicitly grant Nekhlyudov a space to enact his new belief system. In part, the protagonist's homelessness has to do with the author's understanding of his awakening on purely spiritual terms and independent of space and time. At the same time, however, Tolstoy's decision to leave Nekhlyudov homeless at the end also betrays the expiry of the gentry microcosm. Since it turned into a space of corruption and immorality, the spiritual gentry protagonist must conceive of another home for himself that Tolstoy has not given aesthetic form to just yet. Like in Saltykov-Shchedrin's *The Golovlev Family*, Tolstoy's mission in *Resurrection* is primarily destructive—he negates gentry spaces and, in doing so brings the traditional, great nineteenth-century Russian realist novel about gentry life to a close.

CHAPTER 6

REHABILITATING ALL MONSTERS

Love and the Rehumanization of the Grotesque in *The Brothers Karamazov*

Although so far I have been tracing the evolution and expansion of grotesque realism, this otherwise diachronic book departs from chronological faithfulness in this chapter. Instead of ending the story of Russian grotesque realism with *Resurrection*, I end with *The Brothers Karamazov* instead, a novel that, for the first time, both reflects and redeems grotesque realism. If in Goncharov's *Precipice*, society is saved *from* the grotesque, and if, for all of its darkness, Tolstoy's *Anna Karenina* or *Resurrection* is gesturing toward spiritual salvation *from* the grotesque, salvation takes place only *through* the grotesque in *The Brothers Karamazov*. Unlike in all other works of grotesque realism where the body is maligned as a dividing and immoral force, in *The Brothers Karamazov*, the body emerges as a source of healing. For this reason, I break with chronology in this last chapter to provide a counter-model and a narrative of redemption—the kind of narrative that is otherwise virtually absent in other portions of this book. So if *Resurrection* marks the chronological end of this book, *The Brothers Karamazov* marks its conceptual end by yielding some form of reconciliation for the grotesque.

Like other works of grotesque realism discussed thus far, Dostoevsky's *The Brothers Karamazov* zeroes in on the collapse of the gentry family in late nineteenth-century Russia. In the words of Vladimir Goldstein, "The typical nineteenth-century family novel is transformed beyond recognition" in *The Brothers Karamazov.*[1] As a nominally gentry family, the Karamazovs are an aberration—instead of having a home or a nurturing mother, they must endure their father's neglect and abuse while exposed to his immoderate orgies. This picture of familial dysfunction serves as a stage for a series of broader social, political, and ethical questions that Dostoevsky explores about postreform Russia. As the chronicler implies, the disturbed generational history of the Karamazov clan is a reflection of the "senselessness" of the times.[2] Like the moral decay of the Korchagins in Tolstoy's *Resurrection,* the disorder and grotesquery of the Karamazovs spill outwardly from the gentry family to mark a larger societal decline in postreform Russia. Although Dostoevsky does not demonize characters as overtly as in the earlier *Demons* with its antinihilist hues, he reveals the potential for grotesque appearance in many characters in the novel, while also engaging the style's ideas.

The great sensualist of *The Brothers Karamazov,* Fyodor Karamazov, evokes the poetics of corpulence and ugliness typical of the grotesque with his sexual desire and unattractive appearance. Beyond Fyodor, his bastard son, the lackey Smerdyakov, also embodies the grotesque in his physical appearance. Furthermore, a number of other characters either show a potential for grotesque appearance or view others in a grotesque way by objectifying them. The seemingly inherent potential for grotesquery in nearly every character illuminates the fleeting nature of physical beauty and plays an important role in the novel's meditations about active love.

In *The Brothers Karamazov* Dostoevsky uses the grotesque as both a philosophical and an aesthetic category in order to address the limits of active love. As defined by Ivan Karamazov, the grotesque stands for both physical and moral manifestations of ugliness. Grotesque ugliness can strip someone of his or her humanity, turning them into a monstrous other unworthy of active love. Characters like Fyodor Karamazov or Smerdyakov, who embody the gro-

---

1. Goldstein, "Accidental Families and Surrogate Fathers: Richard, Grigory, and Smerdyakov," 92.

2. All citations from Dostoevsky come from Dostoevskii, *Polnoe sobranie sochinenii v tridsati tomakh.* For non-Russian readers, page numbers from Fyodor Dostoevsky, *The Brothers Karamazov,* trans. Richard Pevear and Larissa Volokhonsky, are provided. All subsequent citations for *The Brothers Karamazov* will provide the page number in the translation followed by the volume and page numbers in the Russian edition. Pevear and Volokhonsky, 3; 14:5.

tesque and espouse a grotesque outlook on the world, neither experience nor inspire much spiritual love.

Although the grotesque is often associated with dehumanization and debasement, Dostoevsky also shows us how the grotesque can be rehumanized through love. As Marina Kostalevsky argues, sensuality is a "loaded concept" in *The Brothers Karamazov*—on the one hand it can lead to sin, as in Fyodor's case, while on the other hand it can signify "a passion for life and becom[e] a source of love, including Christian love."[3] In its more sinful and less spiritual incarnation, sensuality falls squarely within the realm of the grotesque. Yet through its dualistic nature, sensuality also presents the possibility for redemption and rehumanization of the grotesque. From this perspective, *The Brothers Karamazov* is quite different from *Anna Karenina* and other novels encountered thus far in this book, books where sensuality is considered irredeemably corrupt and a source for division among people. Whereas Tolstoy's heroine, Anna, only finds isolation in her beauty and in eros, Alyosha Karamazov can participate in active love and discover beauty in everything on earth despite inheriting the deplorable sensuality of his father.

If the grotesque is in the eye of the beholder, then in *The Brothers Karamazov*, Dostoevsky suggests that it can be rehabilitated by a loving gaze. In his Rabelais book, Bakhtin discusses the "power of regeneration" characteristic of the grotesque.[4] He notes the decline of the regenerative component of the grotesque in the nineteenth century, along with a decline in the laughter that sometimes accompanies the style. The tie established between ugliness and Father Zosima's message of love, or between the body, love, and sensuality, brings out this regenerative element missing from other works of Russian grotesque realism. In *The Brothers Karamazov*, the body does not become an impediment to spiritual connection but is rather an integral part of both spiritual love and theological exploration.

I. GROTESQUE INDIVIDUALS

Like in many other works of grotesque realism discussed, the grotesque in *The Brothers Karamazov* begins with depictions of the gentry, particularly the landowner and paterfamilias, Fyodor Karamazov. Scholars have discussed Fyodor Karamazov's persona and especially his physical appearance. Nicknamed Aesop by his sons, Fyodor is appallingly ugly in the fashion of the ancient

---

3. Kostalevsky, "Sensual Mind: The Pain and Pleasure of Thinking," 203.
4. Bakhtin, *Rabelais*, 38.

fabulist.[5] Carol Apollonio describes him as a "remarkably pagan creature" that "dominates the novel," serving as "the great elemental force at its center."[6] As she notes, sensuality and a lifetime of carousing have left their mark on Fyodor's physical appearance. Jackson, who similarly dwells on the character's look, posits that it is the quintessence of *bezobrazie,* which he understands as "the disfiguration of man made in the image and likeness of God."[7] Dostoevsky's narrator foregrounds the character's less-than-perfect exterior, citing his bloated and sagging face. There are "long, fleshy bags" under his eyes, "deep wrinkles on his fat little face . . . a big Adam's apple, fleshy and oblong like a purse" that give Fyodor a "repulsively sensual appearance."[8] Indeed, as Jackson has suggested, there is something distinctly sexual about Fyodor's features, as though "sexual organs [have] metamorphosed into facial forms."[9]

The degradation of a character's face, normally understood as the essence of selfhood and even spirituality, to the level of genitalia, powerfully evokes the grotesque. Fyodor's sagging swollen face, his large lips and hooked nose protrude outwardly to create a disharmonious, grotesque image. Bakhtin, in his discussion of ancient and medieval grotesque texts, cites descriptions of noses as synonymous with those of the phallus,[10] a comparison that Dostoevsky could certainly have also gotten from Gogol. In this sense, Fyodor's ballooning red face serves as a vessel for the frustrated and festering desire of an old man with no avenue for gratification. Fyodor's hooked nose and his mouth with its expulsion of saliva suggest not only openness to the world and its corruption but perhaps also a fruitless ejaculation, a desperate yet foiled attempt to bring forth seed that calls to mind the grotesque body.

With his defiled and defiling face, Fyodor degrades everything to the level of body and sexuality. Until his untimely death, he also espouses a grotesque worldview by lowering the holy and abstract to the level of the body. If Anna Karenina falls on the Hoffmanesque side of the grotesque, then Fyodor is distinctly Rabelasian in his grotesquery. The reader frequently sees him engaging in comic degradation—a key element that Bakhtin associates with the Rabelaisian, Renaissance grotesque. For instance, when Alyosha tells Fyodor that he intends to join the monastery, his father pokes fun at the monastic institution, citing monks who have "monastery wives" to satiate their sexual

5. Jackson, *Close Encounters: Essays on Russian Literature,* 174.

6. Apollonio, *Dostoevsky's Secrets: Reading against the Grain,* 145.

7. Jackson, *Close Encounters,* 172.

8. Dostoevsky, 23; 14:22.

9. Jackson, *Close Encounters,* 188.

10. Bakhtin, *Rabelais,* 86–87, 316.

urges.[11] At other times, such as during the meeting in father Zosima's cell, Fyodor makes similarly crass and degrading comments, bringing the holy and venerated to the level of flesh and vulgarity. He jokes about the elder receiving ladies and inquires about whether females of all species are prohibited in the monastery.

While these examples are fairly lighthearted moments when Fyodor disrupts social decorum, there are also instances in the novel when his grotesque degradation of others takes violent and more disturbing shape, in the form of sexual violation. As Liza Knapp points out, Fyodor's sexual advances toward Alyosha's and Ivan's mother and his desecration of her icon of the Mother of God produce hysterical convulsions and shrieks.[12] Likewise, his implied sexual violation of Stinking Lizaveta indirectly precipitates her death during childbirth.

This last instance of grotesque degradation and violation also facilitates the dissemination of the grotesque past of Fyodor himself. In this case, like in the earlier anti-nihilist novel, the grotesque shapes the portrayal of someone with a mixed social background, the bastard Smerdyakov. If Fyodor's sensuality spreads as a grotesque mentality to his legal sons, his grotesque appearance extends to his implicitly bastard offspring, Smerdyakov. Although the grotesque in *The Brothers Karamazov* may begin with the morally derelict landowner, his sexual depravity perforce also disseminates his grotesquery.

Born on the same day that Grigory and Marfa's child dies, Smerdyakov embodies the hybridity encountered in that child. Since the baby is born with six fingers, Grigory believes that "a confusion of natures" has occurred, making the baby a "dragon."[13] This confusion of natures, which mirrors the hybridity essential to the grotesque as a style, is reflected in Smerdyakov as well. Gary Saul Morson suggests that the character is "a changeling as well as a foundling," who "defies all social categories" while also being "on the margins of the human."[14] As it is implied in the novel, born of the union between a gentry father and the lowly Lizaveta, who is a member of the peasantry or the *meshchane*, Smerdyakov is similarly the quintessential social hybrid.

Indeed, Smerdyakov's hybridity is so deep-seated that it extends beyond the social register. His mother Lizaveta is described as animal-like in her conduct, unusual physical abilities, and general appearance. She jumps fences and goes around barefoot, and the suggestion is that Fyodor raped her only in

11. Dostoevsky, 24; 14:23.

12. Knapp, "Mothers and Sons in The Brothers Karamazov: Our Ladies of Sktoprigonevsk," in *A New Word on* The Brothers Karamazov, 37.

13. Ibid., 95; 14:88.

14. Morson, "Verbal Pollution in *The Brothers Karamazov*," 236–37.

order to prove that his own sensuality was boundless to the point that it could even be aroused by an animal-like creature like Lizaveta. Born of Lizaveta and Fyodor, Smerdyakov is frequently described as somehow subhuman or a hybrid between the human and animal, a "monster" and grotesque outsider to humanity itself. "You are not a human being, you were begotten of bathhouse slime, that's who you are," says Grigory to Smerdyakov in a moment of unusual cruelty.[15] Other individuals, like Fyodor, who persistently refers to Smerdyakov as Balaam's ass, similarly degrade him by describing him as subhuman.

Although belonging to a different side of the grotesque than the sensualist Fyodor, the asexual Smerdyakov is no less a grotesque hybrid than Fyodor. In both his appearance and personality, Smerdyakov displays a muddling of traits. On the one hand, Smerdyakov tries to embody his gentry lineage through fastidious, slow eating like "a fine young sir,"[16] while, on the other hand, he goes around killing cats in the fashion of predatory animals. Further, once he returns from Moscow, Smerdyakov "suddenly became somehow remarkably old, with wrinkles even quite disproportionate to his age, turned sallow, and began to look like a eunuch."[17] The strange aged appearance mixed with his young age, or his gender-ambiguous appearance, hint at Smerdyakov's changeling, grotesque nature.

II. THE GROTESQUE AND THE FAILURE OF LOVE

Both Fyodor Karamazov and Smerdyakov, the novel's two central grotesque outsiders, invite a great deal of abuse. "Why is such a man alive," says Dmitry Karamazov about his father. "No, tell me, can he be allowed to go on dishonoring the earth with himself?"[18] As his later comments reveal, Dmitry's distaste for his father is at least partly motivated by the latter's grotesque appearance. At one point in the novel, Mitya suggests that his father's grotesque ugliness could provoke violence and parricide. "I'm afraid that at that moment his face will suddenly become hateful to me," he says to Alyosha. "I hate his Adam's apple, his nose, his eyes, his shameless sneer. I feel a personal loathing. I may not be able to help myself. . . ."[19] Fyodor thus stands as a grotesque other, similar to the nihilist outsiders in the anti-nihilist novel whose politically and

---

15. Dostoevsky, 124; 14:114.
16. Ibid., 125; 14:115.
17. Ibid.
18. Ibid., 74; 14:69.
19. Ibid., 122; 14:113.

socially subversive status was translated into grotesque sexual deviancy. Like the threatening nihilist who is reduced to a grotesque object, so Fyodor's degradation of the world is met with degradation in return. Instead of seeing his father like a human being, Dmitry's vision of Fyodor is deeply dehumanizing. In Dmitry's gaze, Fyodor is reduced to a collection of grotesque body parts— an Adam's apple, a nose, and eyes.

Smerdyakov is also at the receiving end of a great deal of abuse from all the Karamazov brothers, who not only do not count him as one of their own, but address him by means of derogatory terms such as "lackey" or "monster."[20] Even Alyosha, who is capable of extraordinary kindness, refuses to see Smerdyakov as more than a lackey. At the novel's end, Alyosha places Fyodor's death squarely on Smerdyakov's shoulders, notably saying, "The *lackey* killed [my father], my *brother* is innocent."[21] As Emma Lieber argues, in this sentence Alyosha deliberately renounces any brotherhood ties he might share with Smerdyakov.[22] The chronicler also shares in the distaste for and marginalization of Smerdyakov—he is dismissive of the character as a subject of narration and must make two separate attempts to finally tell Smerdyakov's story.[23]

In a novel that presents powerful messages about active love, the boundaries, inadequacies, and true challenges of human fellowship become especially apparent in the case of Fyodor and Smerdyakov. In the disgust they provoke in others, Fyodor and his bastard son present a significant moral and ethical trial for Father Zosima's broader philosophy of love. Indeed, as some scholars argue focusing on the figure of Smerdyakov, his morally bankrupt nature calls into question the idea that all human beings are "worthy [and] essentially good."[24] The fact that both father and son die through parricide and suicide by the novel's end suggests that they were unloved and perhaps even unlovable, thus challenging the possibility for all-inclusive brotherly love.

This test of active love touches on the broader quandary powerfully advanced by Ivan Karamazov, who insists in his conversation with Alyosha that many people fall short and are unworthy of Christ's love. Ivan invokes the philosophical dimensions of the grotesque as an aesthetic category to make

---

20. Grigory calls Smerdyakov a "monster" (ibid., 125; 14:115), whereas Alyosha and others refer to him as a "lackey" (ibid., 768; 15:189).

21. Ibid., 768; 15:189. Emphasis mine.

22. Lieber, "Smerdyakov and Parricide."

23. As Olga Meerson argues, Smerdyakov's overwhelming stigmatization reads like an ethical test and imperative for the reader who might be the only audience capable of admitting Smerdyakov into the human brotherhood while his real brothers cannot do so. See Meerson, *Dostoevsky's Taboos.*

24. Johnson, "Struggle for Theosis: Smerdyakov as Would-Be Saint," 74.

his argument about unlovable individuals. He tells the story of "some saint," "John the merciful," who spent the night embracing a frozen passerby helping him stay alive by "breathing into his mouth which was foul and festering with some terrible disease."[25] Instead of focusing on the ethical act of salvation in this scene, Ivan degrades the saint's act of mercy and kindness by condemning the foul and festering mouth of the frozen man on aesthetic grounds. In this context, the degradation of the grotesque helps justify the argument that not all humans are lovable.

As Ivan claims, Christ's unconditional love for people is a "miracle impossible on earth" because the awkward or ugly appearance of a person inhibits pure love.[26] He also cites individuals like child abusers, whose moral ugliness would turn into possible exceptions to the Christian ethos of love. Ivan's point is that it is easier to think about doing good deeds or loving mankind in the abstract, because once we are confronted with the person we are trying to help, love and generosity are not sustainable but often give way to disdain or disgust. "If we're to come to love a man," he says, "the man himself should stay hidden, because as soon as he shows his face—love vanishes."[27] Judging by this statement, Ivan's dilemma with loving his fellow man occurs on a fundamentally aesthetic level and is bound up with the grotesque. As an aesthetic category, the grotesque is usually equivalent to ugliness, and it revolves around the body with its various orifices and blemishes. As a result of its ugliness and unseemliness, loving the grotesque can be a true ordeal. It is perhaps only appropriate that some of the most grotesque characters in *The Brothers Karamazov*, like Fyodor Karamazov and Smerdyakov, are dehumanized to the point of appearing completely unlovable.

This tendency toward non-love has an even broader base in the novel as many characters approach others as though they were grotesque objects, degrading them and refusing to extend them any love or empathy. All members of the Karamazov family are especially prone to this warped, grotesque point of view. As the Karamazov brother most resembling Fyodor, Dmitry is driven by passions as powerful as those governing his father's life. Dmitry also espouses a grotesque worldview that lowers everything to the level of body and sexuality by placing his desire for Grushenka above all else. In the process, he dehumanizes his own father and considers parricide acceptable.

We also see traces of this grotesque degradation in Ivan, who at one point expresses to Alyosha that it would not be so terrible if Dmitry were to kill

25. Dostoevsky, 236–37; 14:215.
26. Ibid., 237; 14:215.
27. Ibid.

Fyodor, for one viper would thus eviscerate the other. Ivan's lowering of both his father and his brother to the level of reptiles, just like Dmitry's lowering of himself to the level of a bedbug or his lowering of his father to his ugly Adam's apple, are deeply dehumanizing gestures. Even the saintly Alyosha, despite his characterization as a "chelovekolyubets" [early lover of mankind], is capable of similar degradations of others.[28] When he visits Grushenka, he expects that she will try to seduce him or somehow corrupt his faith, but he is shocked to find human empathy and pity in her. When confronted with her empathy, Alyosha declares himself inferior to Grusha in the ability to love and finds his faith in humanity restored.

As the examples of the Karamazov brothers espousing a grotesque outlook on the world reveal, if Fyodor is the book's grotesque center, then his warped worldview is a family trait that extends to his sons. Although Dmitry, Ivan, or even Alyosha do not bear their father's primal ugliness in their appearances, their outlook is influenced by the same grotesque perspective that abets Fyodor's dehumanization of others. Observing the Karamazov perspective in the novel, one can describe it as a form of synecdochic thinking, or a substitution of a part of a person for the whole.

To use the example of Fyodor, it is his unappealing, swollen face that becomes the epitome of his person under the grotesque gaze of his son and potential parricide Dmitry. Although Dmitry himself evokes the ideas behind holistic vision by believing that God knows his heart and sees the *whole* truth about him, he does not extend his father the same kind of human wholeness he claims for himself. As Jackson argues, in *The Brothers Karamazov* Dostoevsky advances the idea of the whole person, a holistic panorama of a person's actions and intentions that presumably does not allow someone to be "deceived by the diabolical mask of ugliness."[29] In contrast to holistic thinking or even proper synecdochic thinking that reflects the whole in the part, in *The Brothers Karamazov* one is confronted with abortive and coercive synecdochic thinking that gives rise to the deformations of the grotesque.

As a style predicated on the estrangement of reality, the grotesque is especially conducive to a variety of distortions of perception and proportion, including, as Gogol's "The Nose" clearly shows, an emphasis on the part over the whole. Indeed, in his discussion of the style, Bakhtin explicitly emphasizes the exaggeration of individual body parts as an essential component of the grotesque that produces hybridity.[30] As the human forms emerging from plant

28. Ibid., 18; 14:17.

29. Jackson, *Close Encounters,* 220.

30. Bakhtin, *Rabelais,* 26.

stems in the Baths of Titus reveal, grotesque hybridity results from the fragmentation of the whole and the resultant binding of disparate parts together.

In *The Brothers Karamazov,* synecdoche loses its comprehensive, symbolic,
or holistic qualities but rather emerges as random fragmentation and cheap-
ening of a richer whole. In this sense, the emphasis of the part over the whole
might be said to rest on the intersection between synecdoche and metonymy
and the general expectation that a part, any part, can function as a sum total
for the whole. As Dostoevsky's novel indicates, not only do such attempts fail,
but they also do violence to the whole by supplanting it with the offensively
protruding part. Bakhtin cites the potbelly or the phallus as prime examples
of this kind of dysfunctional synecdoche.[31] When someone loses their holistic
identity to become synonymous to a body part, they are dehumanized, turned
into a grotesque hybrid between man and object, no longer a person but a
phallus, a potbelly, or, as in the case of Fyodor Karamazov, an unattractive
Adam's apple.

III. THE UNIVERSALITY OF THE GROTESQUE

In *The Brothers Karamazov,* the grotesque, which serves a social function in
the Russian novel by denoting first the incursion of the social outsider and
then the demise of the socially dominant gentry, assumes a broader ethical
significance. Rather than limiting the grotesque to the gentry family like the
Karamazovs or to the social hybrid, Smerdyakov, Dostoevsky uses the style to
render a wide palette of characters. Although not everyone appears as a grotesque hybrid, Dostoevsky imbues many characters with some small token of
the grotesque, or he at least alludes to their susceptibility to physical deformation and ugliness.

From this perspective, old age is particularly problematized as a great
equalizer in the novel. Several older characters are shown erotically activated,
while being physically unappealing and displaying the swollenness associated with Fyodor. Liza's mother, Madame Khokhlakov, becomes entangled in
romantic flirtations with younger men, and her foot becomes swollen. Con-
valescing in bed with her ailing foot, she also begins to dress more provoca-
tively, prompting even the innocent Alyosha to sense something lewd in her
behavior. Likewise, Grushenka's merchant, Kuzma Samsonov, a man whose
capacity for sensuality is on par with Fyodor's, displays a swollen, grotesque
face. Mitya, who is particularly repulsed by Fyodor's face, is similarly struck

31. Ibid., 26.

by Kuzma Kuzmich's face. Kuzma's face is described as "swollen" while "his lower lip, which had always been thick, now looked like a kind of a drooping pancake."[32] The part supersedes the whole in the portrayal of Kuzma Kuzmich, as his lip is shown grotesquely protruding outward. Besides the grotesque, swollen face, which, like Fyodor's face, similarly recalls genitalia, Kuzma's legs are also swollen from his sickness. By having a broad range of people, including a merchant with no relation to the gentry estate, displaying the same grotesque physical appearance as Fyodor Karamazov, Dostoevsky undercuts social distinctions in the chaos of postreform Russia.

Indeed, it is not only the novel's great sensualists or morally indifferent characters who have a grotesque look. The novel's spiritual center, Father Zosima, is described as overtly unattractive in appearance. We are told that he is "a short, bent little man, with very weak legs," whose "whole face was quite withered, was strewn with little wrinkles." Although Zosima's eyes are said to look like "two bright points," he has very few hairs left, and his lips are as thin as two threads, while his nose resembles a "little bird's beak."[33] Father Zosima may lack the sensual look of Fyodor or Kuzma Kuzmich, but it is clear from Dostoevsky's description that he does not cut an attractive figure; in fact, the text reveals that Myusov disliked him from the start, because there "was something in the elder's face that many other people . . . might have disliked."[34] Zosima may not have a fully grotesque appearance, but his birdlike nose and withered face do not stand up to Ivan's aesthetic expectation for love. In light of the reaction his face produces, Zosima is also someone that can be loved only in the abstract. He himself is aware of the aesthetic challenge Ivan associates with active love and maintains that only those lacking experience in active love fail at it when confronted with a man's unpleasant face.

The fact that a moral character like Father Zosima looks as unappealing as the novel's greatest abusers and most hated sensualists suggests an interesting aesthetic equalization in *The Brothers Karamazov*. Indeed, at one point Dostoevsky explicitly discusses the ephemeral nature of beauty in the context of the novel's most overtly attractive and desirable figure, Grushenka. In the first appearance of Grusha in the text, the chronicler describes her as follows:

> This body perhaps promised the forms of the Venus de Milo, . . . though the proportions must have been and already were somewhat exaggerated. Connoisseurs of Russian feminine beauty could have foretold with certainty,

32. Dostoevsky, 369; 14:334.
33. Ibid., 40; 14:37.
34. Ibid.

looking at Grushenka, that this fresh, still youthful beauty would lose its harmony toward the age of thirty, would grow shapeless, the face itself would
become puffy, wrinkles would very quickly appear around the eyes and on
the forehead, the complexion would turn coarser, ruddier perhaps—the
beauty of a moment, in short, a passing beauty, such as one so often finds
precisely in a Russian woman.[35]

Although Grusha is painted as a true Russian beauty whose appearance
evokes harmony, her attractive look is shown as both imperfect and temporary. However beautiful Grushenka might be in the novel, Dostoevsky's
chronicler suggests that her beauty and the harmony of her features will give
way to disharmony over time. The implication is that Grushenka will succumb
to the powers of gravity, as, over time, her beautifully symmetrical face will
grow lopsided and deformed like the faces of older characters. Grushenka's
susceptibility to aging along with the ugliness that marks older characters,
regardless of whether they are moral or immoral, implies that age may provide balance in the aesthetic dilemmas presented by Ivan. If ugliness becomes
an impediment to love of others, this impediment relates to the natural life
cycle of aging and is relevant when trying to love *anyone*. If ugliness mars the
appearance of everyone, then no one's ugliness should be deemed alien, since
it is ultimately not their pristine beauty but precisely their blemishes that unite
individuals.

This broadening of the grotesque and its meaning in *The Brothers Karamazov* suggests the problematic nature of Ivan's aesthetic preconditions for love.
The expectation that only the beautiful can be loved alienates a large portion
of humanity from active love, while Father Zosima asks that we love everyone and everything, from leaves to all fellow humans. "Brothers, do not be
afraid of men's sin," says Zosima in his homily. "Love man also in his sin, for
his likeness of God's love is the height of love on earth. Love all of God's creation, both the whole of it and every grain of sand. Love every leaf, every ray
of God's light . . . love each thing."[36] This vision of embracing everything and
everyone is fundamentally holistic in nature, the very opposite of the narrow and dehumanizing grotesque worldview that sometimes confronts us in
the novel. Included in Father Zosima's holistic perspective is also the body,
which, whether harmonious or ugly and foul, should be embraced as part of
God's world. If the scope of the grotesque is broad, then the scope of love is
expected to be just as broad if not broader. In fact, we are explicitly told in
the novel's beginning that Father Zosima loves sinners the most. His bow of

35. Ibid., 149; 14:137.
36. Ibid., 319; 14:289.

compassion toward Dmitry at a time when the former is thinking violent and indeed ugly thoughts, and his embrace of Fyodor despite the former's appalling buffoonery, are illustrations of the broad love he advocates. Understanding that we are all ultimately susceptible to rot and ugliness is what allows us to reserve judgment of others.

IV. IS THE GROTESQUE LOVABLE?

Along his theoretical messages of love, it is through the very ugliness and grotesquery of his death that Zosima teaches deeper lessons in *The Brothers Karamazov*. In several of the realist novels discussed thus far, *Cathedral Folk, Anna Karenina,* and *Resurrection,* corpses or dying bodies assume a central role in grotesque realism. The dead or dying body functions as an essential hybrid, denoting the morphing of a human being into a grotesque thing that is no longer human. The decomposing corpse is especially dehumanized and serves as one of the most prominent and possible monsters within the bounds of realism where genuine monsters are by necessity absent. Father Zosima's corpse, although not described at length in the narrative—all we know is that it decomposes—pollutes the air of the novel no differently than the corpse of the merchant fouls Tolstoy's *Resurrection*. In death, Zosima comes to embody the morally nauseating ugliness Ivan believes can become an impediment to love. For the local community, the rapid decomposition of the corpse becomes a test of faith that disputes the legitimacy of the elder's teaching about love. Even the faithful Alyosha is sent into a crisis of faith after smelling the nasty odor.

The rapid decomposition of Zosima's body brings up important questions about the rapport between physicality and the spirit in *The Brothers Karamazov,* questions that Dostoevsky answers rather differently in this novel than in the earlier *Demons*. In her discussion of this part of the book, Liza Knapp argues that Zosima's decay touches on an antinomy in Orthodox thought between those who view the body as a fleshy prison to be transcended and those who view it as part of God's life and therefore integral in salvation.[37] In the earlier *Demons,* under the influence of the anti-materialism of the antinihilist novel, Dostoevsky appears to eschew the physical from his vision of morality. A similar perspective is echoed in Tolstoy's *Anna Karenina* and *Resurrection* where the body is considered as no more than the sarcophagus of the soul and something to be transcended. Yet in *The Brothers Karamazov*

37. Knapp, 200.

Father Zosima embraces the view that the body is integral to salvation and part of God's world. The crisis that Alyosha undergoes concludes with his adoption of Zosima's position through the integration of physicality into his faith.

Zosima's grotesque, foul corpse tests Alyosha's faith, pushing him into an indirect surrender to physicality during his visit to Grushenka, which is initially presented as a spiritual fall. Yet it is during the visit and his purported embrace of the body that Alyosha regains his faith, or rather acquires a broader and stronger faith that does not exclude the physical. He eats sausage at Grushenka's while she sits in his lap, but instead of being led into temptation or the abandonment of spirituality, Alyosha finds human connection. The spiritual bond forged between Grushenka and Alyosha, as well as her kindness and empathy toward him, does not abjure physicality but rather evokes Father Zosima's all-encompassing vision of love. As Terras argues, "It is Aliosha's [sic] spirituality that will save the Karamazovs."[38] While all three brothers share in the sensuality of their father, a Karamazovian spirituality, rooted in earth and flesh rather than abstraction, also emerges in the novel when Alyosha recovers his faith. Instead of closing himself off in a monastery to live a purely spiritual existence cut off from the flesh, Alyosha leaves the confines of the monk's cloister to experience life to the fullest, just as he does with Grushenka. Dmitry's own spiritual awakening at the end of the novel similarly exudes this earthier Karamazovian spirituality.

To return to the tension of part versus whole in the novel, one might say that the experience with Grushenka also affords Alyosha a more holistic worldview. The emphasis placed on Father Zosima's decaying body by the local community is merely another way of emphasizing the part over the whole—as those who lose faith are focusing on a narrow incident instead of remembering Zosima's whole life and teaching. When Alyosha delivers his closing speech at the stone during the novel's conclusion, he speaks from a holistic perspective, bringing up the jubilant Christian themes of "love, reconciliation, and universal brotherhood extending from earth to heaven."[39] It is telling that this closing vision of Christian love does not exclude the body. In fact, we are confronted with another dead body, Ilyusha's. In a gesture of reconciliation, however, Ilyusha's body bears no smell whatsoever. Through this closing image of a pure body, Dostoevsky in a sense rehabilitates Zosima's corpse by providing a holistic picture that shows that bodies do not always smell and one's faith is not always tested. Rather than having grotesque real-

---

38. Terras, *Reading Dostoevsky,* 128.
39. Jackson, "Alyosha's Speech at the Stone: 'The Whole Picture,'" 239.

ism extend to the entire narrative, one can see the grotesque delimited to a few moments that are redeemed by the novel as a whole. The parting image of the children loving their dead friend and one another is a moment of true, exalted, and redemptive beauty—it is also a moment that could be missed if a reader focuses only on the grotesque ugliness of the world.

Indeed, one might argue that at the end of *The Brothers Karamazov*, one finally notices the first stirrings of the regenerative spirit that Bakhtin associates with Renaissance manifestations of grotesque realism. The antinomy between flesh and spirit is obviously predominant in grotesque realism, where the body assumes an essential, though not always positive, role. In the novels by Tolstoy, Saltykov-Shchedrin, Goncharov, Leskov, and even in *Demons*, the emphasis falls on one side of this antinomy, as the body is depicted as being at odds with idealism. In this sense, these novels capture Kayser's darker understanding of the grotesque as a negative style defined by estrangement and loss of spirituality. Yet Bakhtin also articulates a more positive vision of the grotesque in *Rabelais and His World*. As Bakhtin argues, the grotesque becomes a darker style in the nineteenth century, losing its regenerative properties, which are explicitly enacted on the level of the body and physicality.[40] As a result, in the works of grotesque realism we have considered thus far, those who abide by the desires of the flesh are either stripped of their spirituality or their souls are harmed or marginalized. In *The Brothers Karamazov*, however, one can observe for the first time a rehabilitation of the body, and with it the grotesque.

At the end of the novel, Alyosha encourages the grieving boys to eat *bliny* in honor of their lost friend. Initially, Kolya Krasotkin disapproves of the Russian custom of eating pancakes at a funeral, but Alyosha expresses his respect for the tradition and urges the boys to comply. Although the boys are mourning, eating pancakes after the funeral functions as a celebration of life and reconciles the cycles of life and death, a theme persistent throughout the novel. It is perhaps through the eating of pancakes that the boys can accept both the death of Ilyusha and the possibility of Christian harmony. Knapp brings up Bakhtin's argument that eating and banquets are ultimately incompatible with grief, so that by eating after the funeral, the boys and everyone else get some respite from their grief and celebrate "the triumph of life over death."[41]

Through this closing celebration of nourishing the body as a valuable balancing act in the exercise of human grief, Dostoevsky shows the potential for spiritual transcendence and reconciliation through the life of the body so

40. Bakhtin, *Rabelais*, 45.
41. Knapp, 207.

often maligned in other works of grotesque realism. If Father Zosima's body, or Fyodor's and Smerdyakov's repulsive faces, mark the epicenter of the grotesque in *The Brothers Karamazov,* then the novel as a whole redeems these moments of hate and doubt with an overarching vision of love. Flesh and sensuality may present temptation and dehumanization for some, but they also help reaffirm life for others. In the novel's closing celebration, the grotesque is rehumanized through Ilyusha's body, and the banquet implies potential for new beginnings, that "death [can] lea[d] to a new birth."[42]

Through the grotesque realism in *The Brothers Karamazov,* Dostoevsky presents the potential for regeneration that he hints at but does not bring into fruition at the end of *Demons.* When Shatov's legal wife Marie comes back and gives birth to Stavrogin's child, one senses the regenerative potential in *Demons* as well. When the baby is born, it appears as though the degradation produced by Pyotr Stepanovich and others can be redeemed by a new life. However problematic Stavrogin's violation of the marriage ties between Shatov and his wife, the birth of the baby (Stavrogin's baby) provides new hope and new possibility for the estranged Shatovs. Yet after this brief moment of happiness, Shatov is still killed, Kirillov and Stavrogin still commit suicide, and mother and baby still perish from exposure. Despite alluding to its possibility, Dostoevsky leaves no hope for regeneration by the novel's end. In fact, the small window of hope for new life only serves to make the ending to *Demons* all the more harrowing. Within that novel, as he looks at the chaos of postreform Russia, Dostoevsky insists that there can be no new beginning in a world where Pyotr Stepanovich spreads his message of hate and dehumanization and Stavrogin fails in his role as gentry protagonist and moral compass. The physical celebration at the fete at the end of *Demons* is exclusively destructive and does not reflect genuine communion.

In this sense, Dostoevsky's approach to the grotesque in *Demons* mirrors the approach of other writers of grotesque realism. Many works of grotesque realism present the style as a largely negative phenomenon stripped of the possibility for renewal and regeneration. The degradation of the grotesque in works like *The Precipice, Cathedral Folk, Anna Karenina, The Golovlev Family,* and *Resurrection* is not fertile. When rendered through the lens of the grotesque, many gentry protagonists are stripped of their spirituality and consumed by bodily drives. This grotesque vision spells the end of the subject, as

---

42. Bakhtin, *Rabelais,* 283.

far as the reader knows him or her. Whatever semblance of closure or positive ending authors do achieve at the end of their narratives almost always comes in the form of emancipation from the flesh as characters find salvation in the spirit at the exclusion of the polluted and polluting body.

In *The Brothers Karamazov*, however, the body is not denigrated in this same manner. The reconciliation at the end of the novel suggests a rehumanization of the body as an integral part of the human self. As the examples of Alyosha and Dmitry Karamazov reveal, one can be spiritual while still embracing the physicality so essential to the grotesque. In this vein, Dostoevsky's last novel also brings up a different side of the grotesque as a style of renewal. The grotesque appears in Russian realism as a marker of societal change and the degeneration of the privileged gentry class. But where authors of grotesque realism like Tolstoy and Saltykov-Shchedrin construct this degeneration as a form of decline and loss, in *The Brothers Karamazov* it signals possibility and regeneration.

Bakhtin associates the grotesque with degradation, which he defines as simultaneously destructive and regenerative. "Degradation digs a bodily grave for a new birth," writes Bakhtin. "To degrade an object does not imply merely hurling it into a void of nonexistence, into absolute destruction, but to hurl it down to the reproductive lower stratum, the zone in which conception and a new birth take place."[43] The concept of a "new birth" was particularly relevant in late nineteenth-century Russia as the old order was disintegrating and the revolutionaries were cheering for its demise. Aware of the transformative nature of the Great Reforms, Dostoevsky captures the disorder of the times both in *Demons* and in *The Brothers Karamazov*. But where in *Demons* he disparages the disorder of his contemporary Russia with all the virulence of an anti-nihilist writer, in *The Brothers Karamazov* he shows this disorder as productive.

The chaos in the courtroom where peasants and the gentry come together during Mitya's trial is as liberating as it is disorderly. The image of Alyosha, a member of the gentry, dressed in a monk's cassock, and the depictions of Ilyusha's gentry family living in poverty and squalor while the merchant Samsonov prospers, suggest that estate identity is increasingly porous in postreform Russia. If the grotesque aesthetic with which the gentry are painted in other novels signifies, among many other things, the downfall of earlier hierarchies and the inadequacies of the transitional postreform era, in *The Brothers Karamazov* this same aesthetic portends the possibility of something new emerging from the decline of the past. Since everyone is as grotesque as every-

---

43. Ibid., 21.

one else, be they members of the gentry, clergy, or merchantry, then these divisions are surely meaningless. The fellowship of the children at the end of the novel heralds the possibility of a new community made up of equals with no visible social division. This community stands as a future born of the chaos of the Great Reforms at the end of *The Brothers Karamazov*.

THE DEATH OF THE NOVEL

In a country like Russia, which lacked a proper middle class, the gentry and their families were the core demographic for the novel, a genre normally concerned with the middle class. However, as we have seen in this book, in the last three decades of the nineteenth century, portrayals of this key demographic grow increasingly more negative through the idiom of grotesque realism. As the gentry went from being the "soul of the nation" to becoming representatives of its soullessness, the novel genre itself also confronted a dead end. The late nineteenth-century sensuality of the Karamazovs, the beautiful overly sexualized body of the adulterous Anna Karenina, the animalistic world of the Golovlevs, or the amoral and corrupt gentry characters in *Resurrection*—all reflect the collapse of gentry characters. The Karamazovs and Golovlevs also provide compelling case studies for a broader collapse of the gentry family, and so do the Korchagins, the Karenins, and others. The confidence in the gentry at the conclusion of Goncharov's *The Precipice* vanishes in the later part of the nineteenth century as their entire microcosm is shown languishing.

On ethical grounds, the soullessness so often conveyed by the grotesque also meant that the gentry were no longer moral heroes during the late nineteenth century but often became immoral antiheroes. In the famous suppressed chapters of *Demons,* Nikolai Stavrogin seduces a little girl, who reciprocates, and then kills herself. Although the Golovlevs are too primitive to experience significant erotic desire, there is considerable sex outside of marriage in Saltykov-Shchedrin's novel, including the possibility of incestuous attraction. Just as importantly, in that work, parents are callous toward their own children and seem unmoved even by their deaths. Tolstoy's *Resurrection* similarly shows us how the moral decay of the gentry feeds Russia's underbelly of prostitution and the abject poverty of the countryside.

In many respects, the downfall of the gentry and their immorality fit with a broader sense of decline and pessimism that came with the fin de siècle or the end of the century. Max Nordau, who refers to the late nineteenth century as a "dusk of nations," paints a devastating picture: "all suns and all stars are gradually waning, and mankind with all its institutions and creations is perishing in the midst of a dying world."[1] These comments exude the pessimism that defined the fin de siècle in Europe and particularly in Russia where everyone felt exhausted with their reality and experienced vague though unnerving forebodings about the end of the world. In Russian literature, this fin-de-siècle mood began sooner and continued even longer than in the rest of Europe. Grotesque realism is one way in which the realist canon darkened to communicate this deep-seated pessimism. Whether the world was truly dying or not, Russian grotesque realism echoes this sense of a dying society and a declining subject. Although this study ends with the more positive and regenerative grotesque from *The Brothers Karamazov,* the proper chronological conclusion is actually Tolstoy's *Resurrection,* the last novel of the nineteenth century. The image of the decomposing corpse in that work, a subject stripped of its identity and life force, leaves little hope of renewal, but only reinforces the destruction dealt by the dehumanizing conditions of late tsarist Russia.

It is perhaps unsurprising, then, that in telling the story of the disintegration of the gentry and their microcosm, Russian grotesque realism also tells the parallel, metatextual story about its own decline as a genre. One of the things that novels like *The Golovlev Family* or *Resurrection* reveal is that gentry spaces and gentry society are damaged beyond repair. If we trust Dostoevsky's assertion about Russian realism essentially being landowner literature, then this demolition of the gentry world on the page, whether it was also happening in real life or not, had its consequences for the novel.

At the end of Tolstoy's *Resurrection,* Nekhliudov seems trapped in the crossroads, with nowhere to go after his moral awakening because the world

---

1. Nordau, *Degeneration,* 2.

he inhabited beforehand has been exposed as morally bankrupt. The fact that the second half of *Resurrection* is preoccupied with the Siberia travel of the convicts already suggests that Tolstoy has exhausted conventional novelistic spaces. But when Nekhliudov does not find a feeling of belonging with the prisoners and is stranded at the crossroads at the end, the Russian novel itself also seems at a standstill as a genre. Stories, after all, cling to their places and people. While the decline of the gentry may have been at least partly socio-economic, the novel that lionized their demographic was headed for its own parallel decline. As grotesque realism blossomed, it distorted the form of the novel itself, leading to the ultimate "death" of a certain iteration of the genre.

The rootlessness of the novel once invaded by the grotesque is interestingly reflected in a work that arguably serves as an immediate, twentieth-century successor to nineteenth-century Russian grotesque realism—Mikhail Artsybashev's novel *Sanin* (1907). The publication of *Sanin,* which transformed the conventional realist gentry protagonist into a sexual hedonist, was a "cultural event of enormous importance" in fin-de-siècle Russia; it inspired lectures with large audiences, mock trials, and several monographs refuting the "novel's gospel of 'free love.'"[2] In a controversial if not outright scandalous novel that was described as "pornographic," Artsybashev recreated and meditated on some of the same themes of sexual desire and sexlessness but arrived at different conclusions than Tolstoy, Dostoevsky, Goncharov, and others. In the process, Artsybashev proved a fitting successor to the earlier Russian grotesque realism by adopting the poetic of the style without entirely recreating its ideas.

As a writer who came into his own after the blossoming of Russian realism, Artsybashev acknowledged his intellectual debt to realist writers in a 1915 introduction to an English edition of his novel *The Millionaire*: "I am an inveterate realist," he writes, "a disciple of the school of Tolstoi and Dostoevsky, whereas at the present day the so-called Decadents, who are extremely unfamiliar, not to say antipathetic to me, have gained the upper hand in Russia."[3] Despite the significant divergences between Artsybashev's ideas and the works of Tolstoy and Dostoevsky, he engaged in significant dialogue with Russian realism and especially with the poetics of Russian grotesque realism.

Appropriately, the body and how it was understood marked an important point of contention and influence between Artsybashev and his predecessors. Whereas for realist writers the body became the site of the grotesque that encroached upon and deadened the soul with its animal sexuality, for Artsyb-

---

2. Naiman, *Sex in Public: The Incarnation of Early Soviet Ideology,* 47.

3. Artsybashev, *The Millionaire,* 8.

ashev the life of the body was a healthy display of individuality. Artsybashev voiced directly what Russian realist writers expressed only indirectly through the grotesque—namely, that modernization was pulling individuals outside the family and into more individual and non-heteronormative explorations of sexuality. Through his twentieth-century gentry protagonist, Sanin, Artsybashev condemned society's repressive and hollow morality and wholeheartedly embraced sexuality as equivalent to the life force.[4] The implied positive elements of sensuality implicit in Dostoevsky's *The Brothers Karamazov* were overtly expressed in *Sanin*.

Like the nihilist outsiders of the anti-nihilist novel, Artsybashev's Sanin showed no interest in heteronormative conventions of success—marriage or the perpetuation of the gentry family and patrimony. Thinking about human society early in the novel, Sanin declares that many people want "to transform the whole world into a kind of monastic barracks, with one set of rules for everyone based on the annihilation of all personality and the subordination of its power to some mysterious group of elders."[5] The "monastic barracks," which would in effect erase all human sexuality and, indirectly, all human personality, serves as a metaphor for society and its persistent suppression of sexuality's life-giving force. Sanin, who serves as a mouthpiece for his author, celebrates sexuality as eminently healthy. Not only is sexuality not a denial of spiritual identity, but its suppression for the sake of artificial spiritual concerns is treated as an affront to expressions of the self. In a reversal of Tolstoy's depiction of Nekhlyudov's bath rituals as grotesque, Artsybashev provides a positive portrayal of Sanin enjoying his body, stretching and flexing his muscles with pleasure. In this sense, Artsybashev echoes larger fin-de-siècle European trends, as reflected in the work of Max Stirner and Friedrich Nietzsche, who challenged repressive sexual morality and professed the "life-affirming and individualistic philosophy of life that legitimized the pursuit of sensual pleasure."[6] In contrast to earlier Russian realist writers who noted the social eruptions of individual sexuality but used the grotesque to show these impulses as a denial of individual personality and spirituality, Artsybashev anoints sexuality as the site of the self.

Indeed, at one point Sanin seems to specifically refer to the grotesque aesthetic Russian realist writers employed in their depictions of sexuality. "We've

---

4. Lalo, *Libertinage in Russian Culture and Literature,* 145.

5. All references pertain to the Russian edition of *Sanin,* 15. English translations are from *Sanin,* translated by Michael Katz, 19. The translation will be provided first followed by Russian page numbers.

6. Boele, *Erotic Nihilism in Late Imperial Russia: The Case of Mikhail Artsybashev's* Sanin, 11.

stigmatized our sexual desires as bestial," says Sanin. "We've become ashamed of them, and cloaked them in humiliating forms."[7] Might these humiliating forms for authentic and perhaps unavoidable desires be the grotesque aesthetic that Russian realist writers used to paint peripheral sexualities that threatened the nuclear family? For Sanin, and implicitly Artsybashev himself, the sexualized body, although intersecting with the ideological standards of the style, is never grotesque. Instead, Artsybashev uses the grotesque to depict death and dead bodies. Unlike Tolstoy, who believed that indulging in the life of the body precipitated a form of spiritual death, Artsybashev sees the devastation of the body as the only kind of genuine death. "Man is a harmonious combination of body and spirit, until that combination is destroyed [by] . . . the approach of death," says Sanin.

The hybridity found in Russian realism between the human body and the corpse is recreated in *Sanin* but redirected toward death rather than sexuality. The grotesque bodies in *Sanin* are all corpses. It is not the sensualist Sanin that emerges as grotesque but the dying Semenov: in a significant manifestation of the grotesque, Semenov is described as a "terrifying and immobile" grotesque object lacking the animation of the living.[8] Sanin's sister Lida is not considered grotesque as a result of her sexual escapades. Rather, it is only when she considers drowning herself to get out of the predicament of an illegitimate pregnancy that a grotesque image emerges. "Well, and what would happen if you drowned yourself?" Sanin asks Lida. "Good and evil would suffer no loss or gain. Your bloated, disfigured corpse would be covered with silt, then fished out of the water and buried."[9] Like the corpse of the merchant in *Resurrection,* the bloated corpse in *Sanin* serves as a metonymical reflection of society, but, in this case, it reflects societal repression and its death-dealing force.

Whether in Artsybashev's homage to sexuality, Tolstoy's puritanical attitude toward sex, Leskov's anti-materialism, or Dostoevsky's more ambivalent treatment of sensuality, many writers of Russian grotesque realism used the dead body as an essential component of their aesthetic. The dead body in Artsybashev denotes appalling societal repression that renders people lifeless. The corpse is also the quintessential grotesque subject in works by Goncharov, Leskov, Tolstoy, and Dostoevsky, where it serves as a test of faith for characters. As a constant in nineteenth-century narratives of Russian grotesque realism, the dead body warns of the dangers of sexuality and desire. Dead bodies challenged sexual impulses, often equating sex with death and helping

---

7. *Sanin,* Katz, 232; Artsybashev, 231.

8. Ibid., 71; 61–62.

9. Ibid.

characters strengthen their commitment to spirituality. Terrifying in its life-lessness and at times defilement, the corpse captured the dehumanization of late nineteenth-century Russia, showing that life was somewhere else.

The corpse is also metatextually relevant in the history and eventual death of the novel genre. At the end of *Sanin,* which puts an unusual spin on the themes of the novel and strives to perpetuate the storytelling about gentry heroes, Sanin is left on the crossroads just like Nekhliudov. This rootlessness is embraced in both works as potential for change, but it ultimately spells the death of the nineteenth-century Russian realist novel. Therefore, alongside the many decomposing corpses, we also see the eroding frame of the novel. But if the novels I treat are the Russian canon's last great stand, surely they exude the heightening of moral impulses as the genre confronted its own end. In using the grotesque to vehemently expose the dehumanization of the subject in the course of the country's modernization, Russian writers put the style to a pro-foundly humane end. In this sense, we might see grotesque realism as the last moral outcries of a dying genre, the Russian novel, that met its own decline soon enough, but not before proclaiming a broader decline and making one last appeal to humanism and spirituality.

BIBLIOGRAPHY

Afanas'ev, Alexander. "Jurors and Jury Trials in Imperial Russia, 1866–1885." In *Russia's Great Reforms, 1855–1881*. Edited by Ben Eklof, John Bushnell, and Larissa Zakharova, 214–30. Bloomington: Indiana University Press, 1994.

Aksakov, Sergei. *Sobranie sochinenii*, vol. 1. Moskva: Gosudarstvennoe izdatel'stvo Khudozhestvennoi literatury, 1955–56.

———. *Family Chronicle* [*Semeinaya khronika*]. Moscow, 1856.

Alexandrov, Vladimir. *The Limits of Interpretation: The Meanings of Anna Karenina*. Madison: University of Wisconsin Press, 2004.

Apollonio, Carol. *Dostoevsky's Secrets: Reading against the Grain*. Evanston: Northwestern University Press, 2009.

Artsybashev, Mikhail. "Introduction." *The Millionaire*. Translated by Percy Pinkerton, 5–10. New York: B. W. Huebsch, 1915.

———. *Sanin*. St. Petersburg: Zhizn', 1908.

———. *Sanin*. Translated by Michael Katz. Ithaca: Cornell University Press, 2001.

Bakhtin, Mikhail. "Preface to Volume 13: *Resurrection*." Translated by Caryl Emerson. In *Rethinking Bakhtin*. Edited by Gary Saul Morson and Caryl Emerson, 237–58. Evanston: Northwestern University Press, 1989.

———. *Problems of Dostoevsky's Poetics*. Translated by Caryl Emerson. Minneapolis: University of Minnesota Press, 2003.

———. *Rabelais and His World*. Translated by Helene Iswolsky. Bloomington: Indiana University Press, 1984.

Bayley, John. *Tolstoy and the Novel*. New York: Viking Press, 1967.

Becker, Seymour. *Nobility and Privilege in Late Imperial Russia*. DeKalb: Northern Illinois University Press, 1985.

Berdiaev, Nikolai. *The Origin of Russian Communism*. Ann Arbor: University of Michigan Press, 1960.

———. *The Russian Idea*. London: Lindisfarne Press, 1992.

Berlin, Isaiah, Henry Hardy, and Aileen Kelly, eds. *Russian Thinkers*. New York: Penguin Books, 1979.

Blackmur, R. P. "*Anna Karenina*: The Dialectic of Incarnation." *The Kenyon Review* 12, no. 3 (Summer 1950): 433–56.

Blum, Jerome. *The End of the Old Order in Europe*. Princeton: Princeton University Press, 1978.

Boele, Otto. *Erotic Nihilism in Late Imperial Russia: The Case of Mikhail Artsybashev's Sanin*. Madison: University of Wisconsin Press, 2009.

Bowers, Katherine, and Ani Kokobobo, eds. *Russian Writers at the* Fin de Siècle: *Twilight of Realism*. Cambridge: Cambridge University Press, 2015.

Brooks, Peter. *Realist Vision*. New Haven: Yale University Press, 2005.

Catteau, Jacques. *Dostoyevsky and the Process of Literary Creation*. Translated by Audrey Littlewood. Cambridge: Cambridge University Press, 1989.

Chekhov, Anton. *Vishnevyi sad: Komediia v chetyrikh deistviakh*. In *Polnoe sobranie sochinenii i pisem v tridsati tomakh,* vol. 13. Moskva: Nauka, 1974–82.

Chernyshevsky, N. G. *Polnoe sobranie sochinenii v 15ti tomakh*. Moskva: Gosudarstvennoe izdatel'stvo Khodozhestvennoi literatury, 1950.

———. *What Is to Be Done?* Translated by Michael Katz. Ithaca: Cornell University Press, 1989.

———. *Selected Philosophical Essays*. Moscow: Foreign Language Publishing House, 1953.

Clowes, Edith. *Fiction's Overcoat: Russian Literary Culture and the Question of Philosophy*. Ithaca: Cornell University Press, 2004.

Confino, Michael. "The 'Soslovie' (Estate) Paradigm: Reflections on Some Open Questions." *Cahiers du monde russe* 49, no. 4 (Octobre–Décembre 2008): 681–99.

Dostoyevsky, Fyodor. *The Adolescent*. Translated by Richard Pevear and Larissa Volokhonsky. New York: Vintage Books, 2003.

———. *The Brothers Karamazov*. Translated by Richard Pevear and Larissa Volokhonsky. New York: Farrar, Straus and Giroux, 1990.

———. *Demons*. Translated by Richard Pevear and Larissa Volokhonsky. New York: A. A. Knopf, 1994.

———. *The Notebooks for* A Raw Youth. Edited by Edward Wasiolek. Translated by Victor Terras. Chicago: University of Chicago Press, 1969.

———. *Polnoe sobranie sochinenii v tridsati tomakh*. Edited by V. G. Bazanov, F. Ia. Priima, and G. M. Friedlender. Leningrad: Leningradskoe otdelenie Nauka, 1972–90.

Drozd, Andrew. *Chernyshevskii's* What Is to Be Done? *A Reevaluation*. Evanston: Northwestern University Press, 2001.

Durkin, Andrew. *Sergei Aksakov and Russian Pastoral*. New Brunswick, NJ: Rutgers University Press, 1981.

Eekman, Thomas. "Leskov's *At Daggers Drawn* Reconsidered." In *Miscellanea Slavica: To Honour the Memory of Jan M. Meijer*. Edited by B. J. Amsenga, 195–221. Amsterdam: Rodopi, 1983.

Ehre, Milton. *Oblomov and His Creator: Life and Art of Ivan Goncharov*. Princeton: Princeton University Press, 1973.

Eklof, Ben, John Bushnell, and Larissa Zakharova, eds. *Russia's Great Reforms, 1855–1881*. Bloomington: Indiana University Press, 1994.

Elliott, Charles, ed. *The Harvard Classics*, vol. 39. New York: P. F. Collier and Son, 1910.

Emmons, Terence. *The Russian Landed Gentry and the Peasant Emancipation of 1861*. Cambridge: Cambridge University Press, 1866.

Engel, Barbara. *Mothers and Daughters: Women of the Intelligentsia in Nineteenth-Century Russia*. Evanston: Northwestern University Press, 2000.

Engelstein, Laura. *The Keys to Happiness: Sex and the Search for Modernity in* Fin-de-Siècle *Russia*. Ithaca: Cornell University Press, 1992.

Etkind, Alexander. *Internal Colonization: Russia's Imperial Experience*. Cambridge: Polity, 2011.

Fanger, Donald. *Dostoevsky and Romantic Realism: A Study of Dostoevsky in Relation to Balzac, Dickens, and Gogol*. Evanston: Northwestern University Press, 1998.

Field, Daniel. *The End of Serfdom: Nobility and Bureaucracy in Russia, 1855–1861*. Cambridge, MA: Harvard University Press, 1976.

Figes, Orlando. *The Crimean War: A History*. New York: Macmillan, 2010.

Foote, I. P., ed. *Saltykov-Shchedrin's The Golovlyovs: A Critical Companion*. Evanston: Northwestern University Press, 1997.

Foucault, Michel. *The History of Sexuality, Volume One: An Introduction*. New York: Pantheon Books, 1978.

Frank, Joseph. *Dostoevsky: The Miraculous Years, 1865–1871*. Princeton: Princeton University Press, 1995.

———. "The Masks of Stavrogin." *Sewanee Review* 77 (October–December 1969): 660–91.

Freeze, Gregory L. "The Soslovie (Estate) Paradigm and Russian Social History." *The American Historical Review* 91, no. 1 (February 1986): 11–36.

Gibian, George. "The Grotesque in Dostoevsky." *Modern Fiction Studies* 4, no. 3 (1958): 262–70.

Gifford, Henry, and Raymond Williams. "D. H. Lawrence and Anna Karenina: An Exchange of Views." *University of Toronto Varsity Graduate* 12, no. 3 (April 1966): 96–109.

Gogol, Nikolai. *Dead Souls*. Translated by Robert Maguire. New York: Penguin Books, 2004.

Goldstein, Vladimir. "Accidental Families and Surrogate Fathers: Richard, Grigory, and Smerdyakov." In *A New Word on* The Brothers Karamazov. Edited by Robert Louis Jackson, 90–106. Evanston: Northwestern University Press, 2004.

Goncharov, Ivan. *Polnoe sobranie sochinenii v 20-ti tomakh*. Edited by V. A. Kotel'nikov, E. A. Krasnoshchekova, et al., vol. 7. St. Petersburg: Nauka, 2004.

———. *The Precipice*. Translated by Boris Jakim. Ann Arbor: Ardis, 1994.

Goscilo, Helena. "Keeping A-Breast of the Waist-land: Women's Fashion in Early Nineteenth-Century Russia." In *Russia—Women—Culture*. Edited by Helena Goscilo and Beth Holmgren, 31–63. Bloomington: Indiana University Press, 1996.

Gregory, Serge V. "Dostoevsky's *The Devils* and the Antinihilist Novel." *Slavic Review* 38, no. 3 (1979): 444–55.

Grigoryan, Bella. "Noble Farmers: The Provincial Landowner in the Russian Cultural Imagination." PhD Dissertation, Columbia University, 2011.

Gudzii, N. K., and E. A. Maimin. "Roman L. N. Tolstogo *Voskresenie*." In *L. N. Tolstoy Voskresenie*. Edited by N. K. Gudzii and E. A. Maimin, 483–545. Moskva: Nauka, 1964.

Haimson, Leopold, ed. *The Politics of Rural Russia, 1905–1914*. Bloomington: Indiana University Press, 1979.

Harpham, Geoffrey. *On the Grotesque: Strategies of Contradiction in Art and Literature*. Princeton: Princeton University Press, 1982.

Helbling, Robert. *The Power of "Negative" Thinking: The Grotesque in the Modern World*. Salt Lake City: Fredrick William Reynolds Association, 1982.

Holland, Kate. *The Novel in the Age of Disintegration: Dostoevsky and the Problem of Genre in the 1870s*. Evanston: Northwestern University Press, 2013.

———. "The Russian Rougon-Macquart: Degeneration and Biological Determinism in *The Golovlev Family*." In *Russian Writers and the Fin de Siècle: The Twilight of Realism*. Edited by Katherine Bowers and Ani Kokobobo, 15–32. Cambridge: Cambridge University Press, 2015.

Hrushka, Anne. "Love and Slavery: Serfdom, Emancipation, and Family in Tolstoy's Fiction." *The Russian Review* 66, no. 4 (October 2007): 627–46.

Hugo, Victor. *Dramas*, vol. 9. Philadelphia: George Barrie & Son, 1895.

Jackson, Robert Louis. "Alyosha's Speech at the Stone: 'The Whole Picture.'" In *A New Word on The Brothers Karamazov*. Edited by Robert Louis Jackson, 234–53. Evanston: Northwestern University Press, 2004.

———. "On the Ambivalent Beginning of *Anna Karenina*." In *Semantic Analysis of Literature Texts*. Edited by E. de Haard, T. Langerak, and W. G. Weststeijn, 345–52. Amsterdam: Elsevier, 1990.

———. *Close Encounters: Essays on Russian Literature*. Boston: Academic Studies Press, 2013.

———. *Dialogues with Dostoevsky: The Overwhelming Questions*. Stanford: Stanford University Press, 1993.

———. *Dostoevsky's Quest for Form: A Study of His Philosophy of Art*. New Haven: Yale University Press, 1966.

Jahn, Gary. "The Image of the Railroad in *Anna Karenina*." *The Slavic and East European Journal* 25, no. 2 (Summer 1981): 1–10.

———. "Tolstoj's Vision of the Power of Death and 'How Much Land Does a Man Need?'" *The Slavic and East European Journal* 22, no. 4 (Winter 1978): 442–53.

Johnson, Lee D. "Struggle for Theosis: Smerdyakov as Would-Be Saint." In *A New Word on The Brothers Karamazov*. Edited by Robert Louis Jackson, 74–89. Evanston: Northwestern University Press, 2004.

Kaminer, Jenny. "A Mother's Land: Arina Petrovna Golovleva and the Economic Restructuring of the Golovlev Family." *Slavic and Eastern European Journal* 53, no. 4 (Winter 2009): 545–65.

Karamzin, N. M. *Izbrannye sochineniia v dvukh tomakh*. Moscow-Leningrad: Khudozhestvennaia literatura, 1964.

Kayser, Wolfgang. *The Grotesque in Art and Literature*. New York: McGraw-Hill, 1966.

Kelly, Aileen. *Mikhail Bakunin: A Study in the Psychology and Politics of Utopianism*. Oxford: Clarendon Press, 1982.

Knapp, Liza. "Mothers and Sons in *The Brothers Karamazov*: Our Ladies of Sktoprigonevsk," In *A New Word on The Brothers Karamazov*. Edited by Robert Louis Jackson, 31–32. Evanston: Northwestern University Press, 2004.

Kokobobo, Ani. "Corpses of Desire and Convention: Tolstoy's and Artsybashev's Grotesque Realism," In *Russian Writers and the Fin de Siècle: The Twilight of Realism*. Edited by Katherine Bowers and Ani Kokobobo, 162–79. Cambridge: Cambridge University Press, 2015.

Kornilov, Alexander. *Modern Russian History*, vols. 1 and 2. New York: Knopf, 1971.

Kostalevsky, Marina. "Sensual Mind: The Pain and Pleasure of Thinking." In *A New Word on* The Brothers Karamazov. Edited by Robert Louis Jackson, 200–209. Evanston: Northwestern University Press, 2004.

Kramer, Karl D. "Satiric Form in Saltykov-Shchedrin's *Gospoda Golovlevy.*" In *Saltykov-Shchedrin's* The Golovlyovs: *A Critical Companion.* Edited by I. P. Foote, 119–35. Evanston: Northwestern University Press, 1997.

Krasnoshchekova, Elena. *Ivan Aleksandrovich Goncharov: Mir tvorchestva.* Sankt Peterburg: Pushkinskii fond, 1994.

Kurrik, Maire. *Literature and Negation.* New York: Columbia University Press, 1976.

Lalo, Alexei. *Libertinage in Russian Culture and Literature.* Leiden: Brill Publishers, 2011.

Leatherbarrow, William. *A Devil's Vaudeville: The Demonic in Dostoevsky's Major Fiction.* Evanston: Northwestern University Press, 2005.

LeBlanc, Ronald. *Slavic Sins of the Flesh: Food, Sex, and Carnal Appetite in Nineteenth-Century Russian Fiction.* Durham: University of New Hampshire Press, 2009.

Leskov, N. S. *Na nozhakh.* Moskva: Russkaia kniga, 1994.

———. *Sobranie sochinenii v odinnatsati tomakh.* Edited by V. G. Bazanov, B. Ia. Bukhshtab, et al., vol. 4. Moskva: Gosudarstvennoe izdatel'stvo khudozhestvennoi literatury, 1957.

———. *The Cathedral Clergy: A Chronicle.* Translated by Margaret Winchell. Bloomington, Indiana: Slavica, 2010.

Lieber, Emma. "Smerdyakov and Parricide." *Dostoevsky Studies* 19 (2015): 29–32.

Lounsbery, Anne. "Dostoevskii's Geography: Centers, Peripheries, and Networks in *Demons.*" *Slavic Review* 66, no. 2 (Summer 2007): 211–29.

Mandelker, Amy. *Framing Anna Karenina: Tolstoy, the Woman Question, and the Victorian Novel.* Columbus: The Ohio State University Press, 1993.

Manning, Roberta. *The Crisis of the Old Order in Russia: Gentry and Government.* Princeton: Princeton University Press, 1982.

Mann, Iurii. *O groteske v literature.* Moskva: Sovetskii pisatel', 1966.

Matich, Olga. *Erotic Utopia: The Decadent Imagination in Russia's* Fin de Siècle. Madison: University of Wisconsin Press, 2005.

McLean, Hugh. "Resurrection." In *The Cambridge Companion to Tolstoy.* Edited by Donna Orwin, 96–110. Cambridge: Cambridge University Press, 2002.

Meerson, Olga. *Dostoevsky's Taboos.* Dresden: Dresden University Press, 1998.

Meindl, Dieter. *American Fiction and the Metaphysics of the Grotesque.* Columbia: University of Missouri Press, 1996.

Miller, D. A. *The Novel and the Police.* Berkeley: University of California Press, 1988.

Mochul'skii, Konstantin. *Dostoevsky: His Life and Work.* Translated by A. Minihan. Princeton: Princeton University Press, 1967.

Morson, Gary Saul. "Verbal Pollution in *The Brothers Karamazov.*" In *Critical Essays on Dostoevsky.* Edited by Robin Feuer Miller, 234–42. Boston: G. K. Hall, 1986.

Moser, Charles. *Antinihilism of the Russian Novel of the 1860s.* The Hague: Mouton, 1964.

Murav, Harriet. "Maslova's Exorbitant Body." *Tolstoy Studies Journal* 14 (2002): 35–46.

Naiman, Eric. *Sex in Public: The Incarnation of Early Soviet Ideology.* Princeton: Princeton University Press, 1997.

Nechaev, Sergei. "Revolutionary Catechism." In *Assassination and Terrorism*. Edited by David Rapoport, 79–84. Ottawa: Canadian Broadcasting Corporation, 1971.

Newlin, Thomas. *The Voice in the Garden: Andrei Bolotov and the Anxieties of the Russian Pastoral*. Evanston: Northwestern University Press, 2001.

Nordau, Max. *Degeneration*. New York: D. Appleton, 1895.

Opul'skaia, L. D. "Psikhologicheskii analiz v romane 'Voskresenie.'" In *Tolstoy-khudozhnik*. Edited by D. D. Blagoi et al., 314–43. Moskva: Izdatel'stvo akademii nauk USSR, 1961.

Paperno, Irina. *Chernyshevsky and the Age of Realism: A Study in the Semiotics of Behavior*. Stanford: Stanford University Press, 1988.

Pavlova, I. B. *Tema sem'i i roda u Saltykov-Shchedrina v literaturnom kontekste epokhi*. Moskva: IMLI RAN, 1999.

Pisarev, D. I. *Sochineniia*. Moskva: Gosudarstvennoe izdatel'stvo Khudozhestvennoi literatury, 1955–56.

Platt, Kevin. *History in a Grotesque Key: Russian Literature and the Idea of Revolution*. Stanford: Stanford University Press, 1997.

Proffer, Carl. "Introduction: Saltykov-Shchedrin and the Russian Family Novel." In *The Golovlev Family* by M. E. Saltykov-Shchedrin. Translated by Samuel Cioran, ix–xxxiv. Ann Arbor: Ardis, 1977.

Saltykov-Shchedrin, M. E. *Sobranie sochinenii*, vol. 8. Moskva: Gosudarstvennoe izdatel'stvo Khudozhestvennoi literatury, 1969.

———. *Sobranie sochinenii v dvatsati tomakh*, vol. 18. Edited by A. S. Bushmin and V. Ia. Kirpotin. Moskva: Gosudarstvennoe izdatel'stvo Khudozhestvennoi literatury, 1965.

———. *The Golovlev Family*. Translated by Samuel Cioran, ix–xxxiv. Ann Arbor: Ardis, 1977.

———. *History of a Town*. Translated by I. P. Foote. Oxford: Meeuws, 1980.

Saraskina, Liudmila. *"Besy": Roman-Preduprezhdenie*. Moskva: Sovetskii pisatel', 1990.

Scanlan, James. "Nicholas Chernyshevsky and Philosophical Materialism in Russia." *Journal of the History of Philosophy*, no. 1 (January 1970): 65–86.

Senderovich, Savely. "*The Cherry Orchard*: Chekhov's Last Testament." In *Anton Chekhov*. Edited by Harold Bloom, 9–28. New York: Chelsea House Publishers, 2009.

Shklovsky, Victor. *Theory of Prose*. Translated by Benjamin Sher. Elmwood Park, IL: Dalkey Archive Press, 1991.

Solovev, Vladimir. *Lectures on Divine Humanity*. Edited by Boris Yakim. Translated by Peter Zouboff. Hudson, NY: Lindisfarne Press, 1995.

Starygina, N. N. *Russkii roman v situatsii filosofsko-religioznoi polemiki 1860–1870-kh godov*. Moskva: Iazyki slavianskoi kul'tury, 2003.

Terras, Victor. *Reading Dostoevsky*. Madison: University of Wisconsin Press, 1998.

Todd, William Mills, III. "The Anti-Hero with a Thousand Faces: Saltykov-Shchedrin's Porfiry Golovlev." *Studies in the Literary Imagination* 9, no. 1 (Spring 1976): 87–105.

———. "The Ruse of the Russian Novel." *The Novel*, vol. 1: *History, Geography, and Culture*. Edited by Franco Moretti. Princeton: Princeton University Press, 2006.

Todorov, Tsvetan. *The Fantastic: A Structural Approach to a Literary Genre*. Ithaca: Cornell University Press, 1970.

Tolstoy, Lev. *Anna Karenina*. Translated by Richard Pevear and Larissa Volokhonsky. New York: Penguin Books, 2000.

———. *Polnoe sobranie sochinenii, v 90 tomakh, akademicheskoe iubileinoe izdanie*. Moskva: Gosudarstvennoe izdatel'stvo khudozhestvennoi literatury, 1929–64.

Ulam, Adam Bruno. *In the Name of the People: Prophets and Conspirators in Prerevolutionary Russia*. New Brunswick, NJ: Transaction Publishers, 1998.

Venturi, Franco. *Roots of Revolution: A History of the Populist and Socialist Movements in Nineteenth-Century Russia*. Translated by Francis Haskell. New York: Knopf, 1960.

Vinitsky, Ilya. *Ghostly Paradoxes: Modern Spiritualism and Russian Culture in the Age of Realism*. Toronto: University of Toronto Press, 2009.

———. "Russkie dukhi—spiritualisticheskii siuzhet romana N. S. Leskova 'Na nozhakh' v ideologicheskom kontekste 1860-kh godov." *Novoe literaturnoe obozrenie* 87, no. 5 (2007). Accessed online on 10/14/15 at http://magazines.russ.ru/nlo/2007/87/vi10.html.

Vucinich, Alexander. *Darwin in Russian Thought*. Berkeley: University of California Press, 1988.

Wasiolek, Edward. *Tolstoy's Major Fiction*. Chicago: University of Chicago Press, 1978.

Watt, Ian. *The Rise of the English Novel*. Berkeley: University of California Press, 1965.

Weir, Justin. *Leo Tolstoy and the Alibi of Narrative*. New Haven: Yale University Press, 2010.

Wigzell, Faith. "Leskov's Soboryane: A Tale of Good and Evil in the Russian Provinces." *The Modern Language Review* 83, no. 4 (October 1988): 901–10.

Wirtschafter, Elise Kimerling. *Structures of Society: Imperial Russia's "People of Various Ranks."* DeKalb: Northern Illinois University Press, 1994.

Zakharova, Larissa. "Autocracy and the Reforms of 1861–1874 in Russia." In *Russia's Great Reforms, 1855–1881*. Edited by Ben Eklof, John Bushnell, and Larissa Zakharova, 19–39. Bloomington: Indiana University Press, 1994.

Zenkovsky, V. V. *A History of Russian Philosophy*. Translated by George L. Kline, vol. 1. London: Routledge and Kegan Paul, 1953.

Zhdanov, V. A. *Tvorcheskaia istoriia romana L. N. Tolstogo "Voskresenie"; materialy i nabliudeniia*. Moskva: Sovetskii Pisatel', 1960.

INDEX

Adolescent, The (Dostoevsky), 47, 78n2

Aksakov, Sergei: *Family Chronicle*, 18, 79, 81–84, 87–90, 96

Alexander II, 6, 99. *See also* Great Reforms

animal hybridity: as category, 14–15; Chernyshevsky and, 26–27; in Dostoevsky's *Brothers Karamazov*, 121–22; in Dostoevsky's *Demons*, 54–56, 60; in Goncharov's *The Precipice*, 28–30; in Leskov's *Cathedral Folk*, 32–33; in Saltykov-Shchedrin's *Golovlev Family*, 91, 96; in Tolstoy's "On Life," 65

Anna Karenina (Tolstoy): anti-nihilist genre and, 62; beauty and Anna as art object, 68–72; body-soul dichotomy and, 65–68, 74–75; death and the grotesque in, 64–67; dehumanization in, 70, 72–74; Dostoevsky's *Brothers Karamazov* compared to, 119, 120, 129; gentry society and moral decay in, 74–76; *Resurrection* compared to, 71, 75, 98–99, 105, 106, 108, 109, 110, 112; Saltykov-Shchedrin's *Golovlev Family* and, 71, 77, 78–79; sexuality in, 68–69; societal pessimism and anxiety echoed in, 76–77

"The Anthropological Principle in Philosophy" (Chernyshevsky), 25–27

anti-nihilist novels: beginnings of grotesque in, 5; Chernyshevsky's materialism and, 24–27; dead bodies in, 35–36; Dostoevsky's expansion of, 57; key representatives of, 23; materialism, rejection of, 17, 33–34; realism, departure from, 23–24;

religious faith and, 36–37; sexual degradation and objectification of women, 34–35; Tolstoy's *Anna Karenina* and, 62. *See also Cathedral Folk* (Leskov); *Demons* (Dostoevsky); *Precipice, The* (Goncharov)

Apollonio, Carol, 120

Artsybashev, Mikhail: *The Millionaire*, 137; *Sanin*, 137–40

At Daggers Drawn (Leskov), 23, 39, 43

automatons: Hoffman's Olympia, 72; prisoners and Chief Procurator in Tolstoy's *Resurrection*, 104, 113; Saltykov-Shchedrin's *Golovlev Family*, 85–86, 88; Stavrogin in Dostoevsky's *Demons*, 51, 69

Bakhtin, Mikhail: on body parts, 114, 120, 125–26; on degradation, 14, 120, 133; on Dostoevsky's "reduced laughter," 14n50; on the grotesque, 12–13, 73, 110, 131; on grotesque body, 24–25, 55, 90; on regeneration, 119, 131; on soulless marionette, 85; on Tolstoy's *Resurrection*, 99, 102

Baths of Titus, 13, 126

beauty: in Dostoevsky's *Brothers Karamazov*, 127–28; in Dostoevsky's *Demons*, 48–49; in Tolstoy's *Anna Karenina*, 68–72; in Tolstoy's *Resurrection*, 111

Becker, Seymour, 7

Blackmur, R. P., 68

body, human: in Artsybashev's *Sanin*, 137–38; Bakhtin on grotesque body, 24–25, 55,

Printed in Great Britain
by Amazon